Saul Bellow
Drumlin Woodchuck

Saul Bellow
Drumlin Woodchuck

By Mark Harris
/\

The University of Georgia Press · *Athens*

Copyright © 1980 by
the University of Georgia Press
Athens, Georgia 30602

Designed by Richard Hendel
Set in 10 on 13 point Trump Medieval type
Printed in the United States of America

Library of Congress Cataloging in Publication Data

Harris, Mark, 1922–
    Saul Bellow drumlin woodchuck.

    1. Bellow, Saul.   2. Novelists, American—20th
century—Biography.   I. Title.
PS3503.E4488Z675   813'.52 [B]   80-14390
ISBN 0-8203-0529-4

"A Drumlin Woodchuck," from *The Poetry of Robert
Frost* edited by Edward Connery Lathem. Copyright 1936
by Robert Frost. Copyright © 1964 by Lesley Frost
Ballantine. Copyright © 1969 by Holt, Rinehart and
Winston. Reprinted by permission of Holt, Rinehart and
Winston, Publishers.

For Richard G. Stern

Young people, what do you aim to do with the facts about Humboldt, publish articles and further your careers? This is pure capitalism.

Humboldt's Gift

So he lived for many years, with small regular intervals of recuperation, in visible glory, honored by the world, yet in spite of that troubled in spirit, and all the more troubled because no one would take his trouble seriously. What comfort could he possibly need? What more could he possibly wish for? And if some good-natured person, feeling sorry for him, tried to console him by pointing out that his melancholy was probably caused by fasting, it could happen, especially when he had been fasting for some time, that he reacted with an outburst of fury and to the general alarm began to shake the bars of his cage like a wild animal.

Kafka, *A Hunger Artist*

Some old Elizabethan play or poem contains the lines:
". . . Who reads me, when I am ashes,
Is my son in wishes . . ."

Henry Adams, preface to
Mont-Saint-Michel and Chartres

One thing has a shelving bank,
Another a rotting plank,
To give it cozier skies
And make up for its lack of size.

My own strategic retreat
Is where two rocks almost meet,
And still more secure and snug,
A two-door burrow I dug.

With those in mind at my back
I can sit forth exposed to attack
As one who shrewdly pretends
That he and the world are friends.

All we who prefer to live
Have a little whistle we give,
And flash, at the least alarm
We dive down under the farm.

We allow some time for guile
And don't come out for a while
Either to eat or drink.
We take occasion to think.

And if after the hunt goes past
And the double-barreled blast
(Like war and pestilence
And the loss of common sense),

If I can with confidence say
That still for another day,
Or even another year,
I will be there for you, my dear,

It will be because, though small
As measured against the All,
I have been so instinctively thorough
About my crevice and burrow.

Robert Frost, "A Drumlin Woodchuck"

OTHER BOOKS BY MARK HARRIS

It Looked Like For Ever

Short Work of It

Best Father Ever Invented

The Design of Fiction
(with Hester Harris and Josephine Harris)

Killing Everybody

The Goy

Twentyone Twice

Mark the Glove Boy

Friedman & Son

Wake Up, Stupid

A Ticket for a Seamstitch

Something About a Soldier

Bang the Drum Slowly

The Southpaw

City of Discontent

Trumpet to the World

Readers may wish to know which editions of Mr. Bellow's books I have quoted from. I worked from books in the house, familiar to my hand and eye. My choices are not otherwise rational. *Herzog*, *Humboldt's Gift*, and *The Last Analysis* are Viking editions. *Henderson the Rain King*, *Seize the Day*, and *Mr. Sammler's Planet* are soft-cover Fawcett Crest Books. *Dangling Man* is a Signet Book.

M.H.

PUBLISHER'S NOTE

Mr. Saul Bellow, in granting us permission to quote from certain of his letters or other correspondence, has made it clear that he does not in any way endorse this book, nor has he in any way cooperated with the author in its formulation or in its writing. He has concluded, however, that to withhold permission would be to interfere with the conception or plan of this work. For that reason he has granted the use of every passage for which his permission was sought. Grateful acknowledgment is also given to Pamela McCorduck, Ruth Miller, and Richard Stern for permitting the author to reprint correspondence and other writing.

Saul Bellow
Drumlin Woodchuck

Chapter One

I AM IMPATIENT to get forward with this book, and yet I know the value of taking just a little time at the outset to clarify the rules.

The rules: in this book I will quote actual letters. If in any passage I were to alter any expression the reader—you—will be fully advised by signs and signals in common use among scholars and other literate men and women these hundred years or more. I am no "new journalist." Only one kind of journalism exists: good journalism. This is a book of nonfiction, a pure category opposed to pure fiction. No such thing exists under the name nonfiction novel. A thing is not true false. No thing exists by the name prose-poetry.

At all points in this book when I attribute with the usual signs and signals direct speech to any person, the words you will read will therefore be, as far as I am able to make them, the exact words exactly spoken by the person to whom they are attributed. I carry paper and pens with me at all times. I write a diary every night. I keep a journal sometimes. I save all correspondence I receive and copy all correspondence I send. I freely consult the memories of other persons. "Almost certainly, Nachman ran away from the power of his old friend's memory. Herzog persecuted everyone with it. It was a terrible engine. . . . I, with *my* memory—all the dead and the mad are in my custody, and I am the nemesis of the would-be forgotten. I bind others to my feelings, and oppress them."

And oppress myself, too. In this book, as always, I come off worst. It is a device not always appreciated by people who feel that I have hurt them, threatened them, and never acknowledged by critics of my writing, who use against me the facts they would never possess but for me. I am my own instrument or symbol of social criticism.

In this book I will never speak of "sources close" to anyone, nor offer unattributed remarks. I will never hide behind "we" nor shield myself with the passive voice. I will not employ this book or its principal subject in causes not his: I do not volunteer other people's sons for foreign wars. In *Humboldt's Gift* Citrine complains to Thaxter: "You've set yourself up as a Citrine expert and interpret me all over the place—how I function, how little I understand women, all the weaknesses of my character. I don't take that too hard. I'd be glad, though, if you didn't interpret me quite so much. And the words you put into my mouth—that X is a moron, or Y is an imbecile. *I* have no prejudice against X or Y. The one who's out to get 'em is you."

I exert myself to be responsible, though most of my strenuous virtues will never be apparent to anyone but a fellow-writer as sincere as I. I will never tamper with time: everything happens on the day I say it happened, and in the order of reality; if otherwise, I shall clearly indicate the departure. All citations are true, recorded in academic style. I will never say I thought something *then* if I did not think it until afterward: I almost *never* think a thing in the moment—I am too busy writing it down.

Of course, a book compresses reality, condenses time, and abbreviates encounters, except when it inflates, enlarges, or extends those elements. Long or short, whichever way it goes it is a lie. I grant that. But in the everyday sense I do not lie, I tell only the truth as far as I am able.

OFF AT LAST! I have been trying for more than a decade to get off the starting block with my biography of Bellow, and now at last I'm on my way, with many thanks to Professor Richard G. Stern of the University of Chicago, writer, friend. Stern is a bolsterer. From the beginning his enthusiasm has favored possibility. His confidence in me gave me a reality of which I had not been aware. He is far better acquainted than I with the central figure. They have been close friends since the 1950s, colleagues, neighbors. Stern knew that I must go on, even when I was most doubtful.

In my making of this book Saul Bellow, on the other hand, has been of no assistance. How wise he was! How shrewdly he read my character, how thoroughly he tested me! I had been untrustworthy, not so much for reasons of bad character but because I did not know what he wanted me to be—what things he admired in the world—and the reason I did not know what he wanted me to be was that I did not know what he was.

I attributed his mistrust of me to deficiencies of his character. I assumed he was eccentric, temperamental, and unreasonable, as artists are said to be. I was yet to learn, by my study of Bellow, that an artist could remain alive only by resisting every effort to make him into a monument. "Humboldt! My goofy sister named him after a statue in Central Park."

Because he mistrusted me I learned to seek in myself those aspects of myself he mistrusted, not merely to deny them but to see if they were really there, and when I found them I was able to deal with them, and to become better. Frost had done the same for me—held me off, forced me to focus my thought upon him, forced me to ask myself why he resisted me. I had gone in the very beginning directly from Frost to Bellow, Vermont to Tivoli, as we shall see.

Bellow saw from experience the dangers to which I was susceptible, the traps into which he had seen others fall who had come toward him to share something of him they wanted—an aura, a wisdom glowing—whose real intention might have been to use him for their own gain or fame, place or position. He was yet to speak of people with their thumbprints on his windpipe. He had come to be mistrustful of individuals, seeing their opportunism as unfortunate but real, and he became, to save himself, not angry with them but only difficult, recalcitrant, reluctant, a foot-dragger, a woodchuck whose mind was a memory-bank of holes to run into, so that every encounter with Bellow was bound to be attended by the merest impossible obstacles of time, place, logistics, a connection missed, a wallet lost, persons detained, telephones unanswered, evasion, escape, everything clouded by the simpler forms of misunderstanding.

It was his way of freeing his mind and remaining flesh. No biographical monument for him. He was still "groping," he insisted. Not yet "*fini.*" Writers, he once wrote, "are often transformed into Major Literary Figures and for the rest of their lives do little more than give solemn interviews to prestigious journals or serve on White House committees or fly to the Bermudas to participate in international panel discussions on the crisis in the arts. Often the writer is absorbed by the literary figure. In such cases it is the social struggle that has been most important, not the art."[1]

Why art? Isn't the "social struggle" more important? On this subject Bellow has quoted someone else: "The remedy is the poem itself. Art is the community's medicine for the worst disease of mind, the corruption of consciousness."[2]

IN TIME I saw how real those things were which Bellow valued. This required some years, some travel, some postage, some exasperation, and a great deal of repeated reading in the work of Bellow; and when I was done I knew that I had improved myself by providing myself with a model of a man who had resisted many temptations. I grew up to a belief in his character. He ceased to be eccentric. "Success" did not spoil him but only strengthened him. At a peak of "success," after *Herzog* (after which all his books were reissued as if "by the celebrated author of *Herzog*"—so said the publishers' advertising), he saw with the clearest eye, and so wrote on the most public wall, "We have at present a large literary community and something we can call, *faute de mieux*, a literary culture, in my opinion a very bad one."[3] He could never be bribed to change his mind. One might have thought that the very man acknowledged (not by himself) as a leader of the literary culture would therefore have been an American booster. But not our difficult Bellow, truthful at all cost, going forward with his work in spite of fads and fashions, never stepping from his path to suit the trade. He was one who learned from history.

This is a book about a man whose talent expresses hope. In a cynical world we are skeptical. A great deal of literary work sneers at the world, destroys life, kills. Bellow yearns for the salvation of the world, risking himself to balance cynicism with his hope. A thousand times painful therefore to hear him accused of cynicism. He is accused of having made a great deal of money. Therefore he wrote for money?

People who say such things are almost always people writing for

1. *The Arts and the Public*, ed. James E. Miller, Jr., and Paul D. Herring (Chicago: University of Chicago Press, 1967), p. 17.
2. "Culture Now: Some Animadversions, Some Laughs," *Modern Occasions*, Winter 1971, p. 178.
3. "Cloister Culture," *The Best of "Speaking of Books*," ed. Francis Brown (New York: Holt, Rinehart and Winston, 1969), p. 5.

money only. They cannot imagine another kind of writer any more than they can imagine another kind of world. Here is an example of the cynicism I am talking about: I was flying for the Peace Corps from New York to Senegal shortly after the publication of *Herzog*. In those days I could not sleep on airplanes. It was the middle of the night. Beside me a black Pentecost missionary minister named Miss Johnson, blissfully sleeping, dreaming of the Kingdom of Heaven. Hunched under my little high-intensity light I read the PanAm copy of *The New Yorker* for January 9, 1965, containing a short bitter essay by one Thomas Meehan, called "Claus (A Leftover Candy Cane for Mr. Saul Bellow)." Some of its best phrases were stolen from *Herzog*, and yet the essay was an attack upon that book, or certainly upon its author, for being "woebegone, intellectual . . . long-winded . . . melancholy," and finally "uninteresting." These are subjective judgments that may describe nothing more than Mr. Meehan, who ought to understand that accusations of motive are very likely projections of one's own. Meehan's conclusion infuriated me. "With this thought in mind," Meehan ended his essay, "he [Herzog] fell into a long winter's sleep, as visions of sugarplums, paperback rights, a six-figure sale to Joseph E. Levine, and the New York *Times* best-seller list danced in his head." Whose head?

Had I not been in an airplane over the Atlantic I would have telephoned Mr. Meehan and abused him. Bellow, in pain, created literature; for the moment *Herzog*. Meehan, denying his own pain, attacks the maker of the book.

HERE IS ANOTHER experience of bitterness. At the University of Minnesota, where I was a graduate student from 1951 to 1954, I had a friend who claimed an acquaintance with Bellow. Bellow had been a young teacher there in the late 1940s (again in the 50s), and I heard something about him from teachers and students who had seen him coming and going. I eagerly listened. I was myself becoming a writer and I cared to know how writers lived and walked and talked. It seemed to me a good omen that Bellow had had an office in the very building where mine was—Temporary North of Mines, "a temporary wooden structure to the north of the School of Mines. From the window we saw a gully, a parking lot, and many disheartening cars."[4]

4. "John Berryman," foreword by Bellow to John Berryman's *Recovery* (New York: Farrar, Straus and Giroux, 1973), p. ix.

My friend was theoretically filled with good will for all sorts and kinds and races and colors of men women and children, a student of literature and of the politics of history, a deep reader, overcome by a reverence for books and for almost anything else printed on a printing press. This is not to say he agreed with everything he read. He fought back. To living journals he wrote letters, and those letters in turn he himself printed, sending them to me for years afterward in lieu of personal messages, making me party to his disputes with *The New Leader* and the Minneapolis *Tribune*.

Quotations from journalistic editorials began to replace speech in his mouth. It was a humble affliction, a modesty about his own views, not a bad thing, and he might have led a serene and fulfilling life with his wonderful family, working by day, reading by night, had his humility not turned to bitterness.

And so he became a man who could detect in every event only the element of impurity, however small, and dwell upon it, and elevate the fractional impurity to the level of the whole. A work of fiction he could see only as the writer's deception for bad purposes—"You hide behind your characters with your filthy ideas," he said. His meanness increased. In the short space of twenty years, from the time I knew him to the moment of my most recent word of him, he became an adherent of the most conservative Establishmentarianism compounded by evangelism, renouncing the socialist ideals of his youth. Of course he discovered that old run-of-the-mill anti-Semitism. Bellow drew the type in *Mr. Sammler's Planet*—Cieslakiewicz, caretaker of the cemetery, who saved Sammler from capture and death. But then, strangely, "after some years, the letters began to contain anti-Semitic sentiments. Nothing very vicious. Only a touch of the old stuff."

I date my friend's decline from 1953, the year *The Adventures of Augie March* burst upon us. The "success" of *Augie* drove him wild. One day he flew into a rage which at first appeared to me to be unconnected to the words he spoke: "I sat beside him in the barber shop." Meaning what? Go on. He did not go on. It was the end. So wholly had his passion subdued him that his logic failed him: having said nothing, he thought he had said everything.

What he meant was this: *I once sat beside Bellow in the barber shop close enough to see that he was only human like you and me.* After all, Bellow had been *printed*. Two books by then, and now *Augie*. My friend thought God should identify a printed man, especially if the man was destined to arrive on the best-seller list. He should be obvious. He should not require a haircut. Maybe only a trim. Although Bellow never claimed any humanity for himself above ordinary membership, my friend claimed it for him, and condemned him for failing to fulfill such expectations, and branched out from Bellow to anyone else who might have been more or less "successful," and at the same time took up God, too, although God had already filled him with confusion by neglecting to stamp the secular seal on those children Published or otherwise Chosen. In the end my friend condemned the whole world wherever it survived, and wished death upon everyone at last in his friendly way.

ON THE OTHER HAND—on the brighter side, one might say—I am thinking of a dark and beautiful professor beside whom I sat at a dinner party in San Francisco on the night of March 10, 1967, who told me that she had recently seen Bellow, who was then (she said) occupying a house in southern California. Said she, "The whole cast of *Herzog* was there." I had by that time become warmly attached to my idea for a biography of Bellow, and I therefore took her information into my possession, more or less correcting its hyperbole: reducing the "whole cast" to Bellow and her, I concluded that they had spent some time together in southern California. Afterward, however, when I mentioned her to Bellow, he said he did not know her.

Later that year a moment occurred which was a companion to the first. I encountered the dark and beautiful professor at the Palmer House in Chicago, at a meeting of the Modern Language Association. She said, "I've just come from having a drink with Saul Bellow." But when I encountered Bellow that evening he said no, he had not had a drink with her, they had talked on the telephone. "Maybe," said he, "she was having a drink at her end and I was having one at mine."

Writers walk around in other people's fantasies, nightmares, psychiatric sessions. Sometimes they are really there, and sometimes they are not. The professor from San Francisco State University imagined herself drinking with Bellow in a house in southern California. Or else she *was* there, and so was he, and they did drink.

OF ANOTHER LADY'S STORY I am more certain. I met her first in 1953. She was an important person to me, since it was through her that I established my own first living connection with Bellow. She was Catherine Lindsay, and she told me that she was Lily in *Henderson the Rain King*. True, she was one of "these big beauties," as Henderson calls her—"I hadn't seen her in more than a year, not since I put her on that train for Paris, but we were immediately on the old terms of familiarity just as before. Her large, pure face was the same as ever. It would never be steady but it was beautiful. Only she had dyed her hair. It was now orange, which was not necessary, and it was parted from the middle of her forehead like the two panels of a curtain. It's the curse of these big beauties sometimes that they are short on taste. Also she had done something with mascara to her eyes so that they were no longer of equal length. What are you supposed to do if such a person is 'the same as ever'? And what are you supposed to think when this tall woman, nearly six feet, in a kind of green plush suit like the stuff they used to have in Pullman cars and high heels, sways; and in one look she throws away all the principles of behavior observed on 57th Street—as if throwing off the plush suit and hat and blouse and stockings and girdle to the winds and crying, 'Gene! My life is misery without you'?"

Once, with the poet John Berryman, Bellow writes, "as we were discussing Rilke I interrupted to ask whether he had, the other night, somewhere in the Village, pushed a lady down a flight of stairs.

" 'Whom?'

" 'Beautiful Catherine, the big girl I introduced you to.'

" 'Did I do that? I wonder why?'

" 'Because she wouldn't let you into the apartment.'

"He took a polite interest in this information. 'That I was in the City at all is news to me.' "[5]

In 1959 beautiful Catherine sought employment in our department at San Francisco State, and Bellow had written for her a letter of reference so affecting me that I instantly sat down and wrote one to *him*: "I have been thinking of you all day because my boss showed me this morning the letter you wrote on behalf of Catherine Lindsay. Letters like that are impossible to write, but you did it. I think Catherine will be hired." I continued, taking this occasion to unload some of my troubles. "I have been reading galleys of a novel I

5. Ibid., p. x.

thought was funny when I sent it to Knopf, but in galleys there is nothing to make me laugh. . . . Now I must go on and find something new to write about, but I feel heavy, and I wonder where the new experience is to come from. I seem to have overtaken myself, having written myself up-to-date, so that instead of some larger thing looming for me there seems to be only something smaller and narrower ahead. I can go on doing the same old thing, but this is what writers mostly do, and I don't want to be the kind of writer there has mostly been."

From Minneapolis, Bellow replied in the most encouraging terms: "I'm glad you wrote me a letter. It's silly not to know each other, isn't it? We've crossed the same ground any number of times and besides I have a sympathetic impression of you. I know very well— all too well—what you mean when you say you've overtaken yourself. You can't, really, except within a given system which makes repetition inevitable. But then it's not so much yourself you're repeating as it is a way, a system, a procedure, a method which originated with certain old gentlemen in France, England, Russia. So let's say you've overtaken Turgenieff (for example). I don't know your work well enough to say this. Let's assume I'm speaking of myself. Without an influx of new life the situation becomes depressing in the extreme, as it was in the end for Turgenieff himself. Once more a woman who loves, in the same old way; once more a lazy nobleman. The benefits of a literary education soon come to an end. Is this what you're talking about? Or is it only what I am making of it? . . .

"You'll like Catherine Lindsay. I hope she gets the job."

I had been made joyful by his letter. For several months we briskly corresponded. I hoped that I would meet him. In July I wrote to him in praise of *Henderson the Rain King*, which appeared that year. Ever afterward, when I enjoyed reading a new work of his I wrote to tell him so. Thus I wrote him after every work, for all his work delighted me, struck me right. I speak for myself only. I make no scientific critical claim for his objective worth. Perhaps I admired his growing each time stronger, surpassing himself, or perhaps it was only the pleasure I felt in his versatility: even when a story or novel slowed, lost force, slid into doldrums, its language and images carried it until a fresh wind rose. He seemed to me always funny, moving, even when I was unable to follow his philosophical gyrations, or didn't care, or felt like telling him, as Renata told Citrine, "You'll wind up with bare feet in the Loop carrying one of those where-will-you-spend-eternity signs." I admired his craftsmanship and knew the labor of it. "The fitting together of the parts gave me the pleasure of a good intricacy."[6] Bellow was story-teller and world-saver, and I admired that ambition. Life, peace, and civilization he favored, guns and untimely death he opposed. Historian, humorist, Jewish, American. A political radical, seeing the world whole, true anti-fascist, he made me want to write better, he enlarged and extended my imagination, my vocabulary, my consciousness, and my idea of the English sentence.

He replied to my letter, inviting me to submit work to his new magazine, *The Noble Savage*. I sent him a story of mine I had been unable to publish elsewhere, and he published it, paying me two hundred and fifty dollars. He was associated with several magazines, but none survived. Charlie Citrine had high hopes for *The Ark*, but it cost him money beyond his means, and Renata challenged his motives: "Who needs this Ark of yours, Charlie, and who are these animals you're gonna save? You're not really such an idealist—you're full of hostility, dying to attack a lot of people in your very own magazine and insult everyone right and left."

In September—still 1959—he wrote me again from Minneapolis, commenting on that novel of mine which had disappointed me in galley proofs. His insight into my book was helpful to me also as light upon myself: the book was a "switch," he wrote, "on the engaging and seemingly open and gay character who however has qualities not to be openly shown, so that the openness is the greatest feint of all."

Beautiful Catherine Lindsay got the job, and Bellow for some reason fled the country. Often he left when a book appeared, lying low until the tide of reviews had ceased. "In very great haste," he wrote to me November 12, 1959, "because I'm leaving for Europe and that's not the worst of it. . . ." ("So you're going to Europe," says big-brother Julius to Charlie Citrine. "Any special reason? Are you on a job? Or just running, as usual? You never go alone, always with some bim. What kind of cunt is taking you this time?") I don't know whom he went with, if anyone, or why. Some years afterward he told me that he had that year received a grant from the Ford Foundation,

6. *Humboldt's Gift.*

and that his (then) wife had obtained for him a State Department grant to tour the world speaking: while he was on tour around the world she stayed home and spent his Ford grant. From Rome early in 1960 he sent me a postcard commiserating with me on the death of my father: "When my father died I was for a long time *sunk*. I hope you're a wiser sufferer. Our business is survival, with pain unavoidable. By now I'm far better." And soon afterward: "I'd never have come here if home hadn't blown up under me. Now I'm well enough to think again. I'm all right. . . . Give regards to C. Lindsay. How is she? From darkest Yugoslavia."

For more than a year, no word. Finally I actually met him.

IN VERMONT, for *Life* magazine, and ultimately for my own writer's education, I spent August 17 and 18, 1961, making notes as fast as I could type them while Robert Frost talked, and August 19 driving a rented car from Vermont to Tivoli, New York, Frost to Bellow.

At a nice little bookstore in Vermont I had purchased a slim book called *The Writer's Dilemma*, containing Bellow's essay "The Sealed Treasure," telling of a drive he had taken through Illinois "to gather material for an article." I read his essay at a coffee-stop. By the "sealed treasure" Bellow meant "the intelligence or cultivation" of women of small towns, whose "private vice" was reading great books from the local public libraries. Their connection to the great world of spacious feeling beyond Shawneetown was the local library. "I went to the libraries and was not surprised to learn that good books were very much in demand, and that there were people in central Illinois who read Plato, Tocqueville, Proust and Robert Frost. . . . The writer's art appears to be a compensation for the hopelessness or meanness of existence. *He* by some method has retained the feelings and the ideal conceptions of which no sign remains in ordinary existence." Here he cited Vachel Lindsay, "preaching the Gospel of Beauty and calling on the people to build the New Jerusalem." I had written a book about Lindsay nine years earlier, which Bellow had admired. Then, too, his balanced politics, poised between hope and despair: "Yes, there are good reasons for revulsion and fear. But revulsion and fear impair judgement. Anxiety destroys scale and suffering makes us lose perspective. One would have to be optimistic to the point of imbecility to raise the standard of pure Affirmation and cry, 'Yea, Yea,' shrilly against the deep background of 'Nays.' But the sympathetic heart is sometimes broken, sometimes not. It is reckless to say 'broken'; it is nonsense to say 'whole and unimpaired.' On either side we have the black and white of paranoia."[7]

And so I drove up to the lawn at the house at Tivoli in the Hudson Valley. I made photographs of Bellow and his son Adam on the same roll of film with which I'd shot Frost, and I slept in a clean bed on a hot night beneath a sheet only, and in another room of that vast and marvelous house Bellow, and somewhere Adam, and in yet another room a gentleman friend of Bellow's who worked for the government, and somewhere in some room or other (I never knew where) slept or lay a woman of extraordinary beauty. My not knowing where she was made me restless. To this day I do not know where she was, or who—I made no notes on Tivoli: my head was filled not with Bellow but with Frost.

Bellow cooked dinner for me, and for some reason we ate alone (I suppose because I had arrived late), and afterward he read to me from a work in progress which became the novel *Herzog*. I have never been able to find or remember the sections he read (perhaps they never reached print), although I do remember that he wore a hat while he read—charming eccentricity, I thought, until, seven years later, my age then his, my eyes undergoing changes, I concluded that his hat might have been a shade against the light. (Herzog "put on his fedora, as if he hoped to derive some authority from it.")

Of course I chattered on about Frost. Late that year, after my article appeared, Bellow wrote to me about it. "Very much liked your Sandburg-Frost article. How neatly you let Sandburg portray himself. One or two strokes of the dollar sign and the thing was done. Frost is a different kettle of woodchuck altogether. Woodchuck I say because he has more exits to his burrow than any man can count."

I remember best of all—better even than the woman who was the guest of the house—standing at a window with Bellow and feeling fearful of the silence, the solitude of his surroundings, and remarking, "I'd be nervous. Do you own a gun?"

"No," he beautifully replied, "why should somebody die because I'm nervous?"

In Bellow, only crazy people carry guns, shooting a cat in the attic, shooting through the telephone directory on a music stand. Hender-

7. *The Writer's Dilemma* (London: Oxford University Press, 1961).

son, recovering from craziness, gives up hunting—"it seemed a strange way to relate to nature." "But I couldn't see what good it would do me to fire a gun," says Charlie Citrine. "As if I could shoot my way out of my perplexities—the chief perplexity being my character!" Through all Bellow's work violence is pointless, mad, associated with futility and brainlessness.

From Tivoli, on Sunday, I left for New York City. Later in the week Bellow came down. I dined on Wednesday with Bellow and my friend Herbert Blau at a restaurant called Oscar's on Third Avenue, passing from there with Bellow to a lady's apartment. I hoped it would be the lady I had pondered in the night at Tivoli, but it was not, though it was another as fine; and met there Bellow's first son, Gregory, in his teens. So I saw Bellow Saturday, Sunday, and Wednesday, but not again for four and a half years.

I had gone to Bellow at Tivoli in purity, without motive. It did not occur to me that someday I might want to write his biography or anybody else's. I was essentially a novelist—now and then a journalist. Four years later, however, it occurred to me to write an article about him for *Life*—the Frost had turned out so well—but when I wrote to him he replied: "Thank you for your offer, it's a very good one. But the fact of the matter is that I've had about all the public attention I can safely absorb. Anyone who held a geiger counter on me now would hear a terrible rattling. I liked your Frost and Sandburg piece . . . but somehow I think I would be ill-advised to spread myself all over Life even under your auspices. What I want to do now is to lie low and gather a little shadow. . . . Please remember me to Wright Morris. I didn't much care for his last book. Regrettably I told him what I thought of it and I appear to have blown up a valuable friendship. Odd, but I don't number so many friends among writers now. There was a time when we loved one another. No one gives me the time of day anymore except yourself, and John Cheever and I forget who else. The rest have vanished."

I SAW HIM NEXT at his apartment in Chicago on South Shore Drive, and his wife, Susan, who was neither the woman of Tivoli nor the woman of Manhattan but someone other, whose olive beauty made me restless. Her trousers snugly fit her hips; and Daniel, who was Bellow's third son, even as Susan was his third wife; and our mutual friend Richard Stern.

Once again I was on journalistic assignment, this time for *Sports*

Going the way I must go, I'm willing to ride with it. Great biography may be creative, too, and I have here a very short list of only three names—of which yours is one—of my contemporaries, whose biographies I should like to write. It is the same list I had in mind in January, when I visited your house, but I hesitated to mention the matter for precisely the reasons I hesitate now: reasons of doubt; is it right for me to do?

I want only to ask now, as I've asked my other potential subjects (Blau and Irving), that you not say No to me now, nor Yes to someone else, until I have a chance to present my case in person.

And so, of course, to present my case in person I must go to Chicago where Bellow was. Meanwhile, after seeing a program in London of three one-act plays by Bellow, I wrote to him to tell him my impressions. He did not reply to that letter. I sent him a copy of a new book of mine, just published, but he did not acknowledge receiving it.

Anyone who can ignore his mail wins my admiration. Bellow writes that Oscar Wilde "had known a promising young man who had ruined himself through the vice of answering letters."[8] Stern has told me that Bellow receives "torrents" of mail, that he once ignored six telegrams from a college seeking to honor him. Not his biography but his work occupied Bellow. His art. What is art? Robert Frost called a poem "a momentary stay against confusion." Bellow quotes Henry James: "the cure of souls." What can art tell? "Well," replies Bellow's man Henderson, "for instance, that chaos doesn't run the whole show. That this is not a sick and hasty ride, helpless, through a dream into oblivion. No, sir! It can be arrested by a thing or two. By art, for instance. The speed is checked, the time is redivided." He was busy. He was at work. Why should he have answered my mail? Never mind, I went to him.

8. "Reflections," *The New Yorker*, July 19, 1976, p. 62.

Chapter Two

I ARRIVED by air in Chicago on the afternoon of March 23 and traveled by taxicab to the Del Prado Hotel on the South Side. For some reason, the taxicab driver believed I was a physician, but when I told him I could not solve his medical problem (a tricky version of venereal disease) he began to describe for me in rich and colorful language the corruption of the city. Throughout most of the drive he was cheerful and loquacious, but during the last few minutes he became unaccountably sullen.

In the hotel I instantly telephoned Bellow to arrange to meet with him to talk about my letter from France. I telephoned him at his home. Yet I must have known that he would not be there because I had heard of his separation from his memorable and beautiful wife, Susan. Therefore it must have been Susan I wished to speak to. I remembered that she had worn dark pants fitting snugly, and her face shone. Her hips I remembered. And her lips. Hips and lips. A portrait of beauty, health, and happiness, and I had assumed that after two mistaken marriages Bellow had formed with her a bond to last forever.

Greetings. Casual talk. I asked for Bellow. Susan said that he was "probably this very minute walking in the door at Morton's Steak House," where he had gone to dinner with his son Gregory. I asked when he would return. She said she did not know when he would return, that in fact she did not know if she would see him again that evening; no, she did not expect to see him, he had been there to see

Daniel—she was flustered—sometimes she was more certain of his hours than at other times, or of his days . . . "Mark!" she said, deciding not to prolong things (her sharp, crackling firing-off of my name made my heart leap), delivering shocking news with speed, to reduce its impact—"Mark! Saul and I are separated."

I felt a kind of satisfaction to hear this, because Bellow had not replied to my letter from France, which had not been, after all, a simple letter dashed off on my summer vacation, but a very serious letter proposing to invest a great portion of my life in his. My satisfaction illuminated me at other levels. Failure humanized him, as if he were sitting in the chair beside me in the Minneapolis barber shop. We cheer for people on the way "up," but when they get there we throw rocks at them. ("The crowd razzed him as he acknowledged at last that this was beyond his strength. He simply couldn't do it. And I rejoiced at the guy's failure. Which is a hell of a thing to admit, but it happens to be the case.")[1] We welcome the humility one will acquire from a dose of everyday trouble.

In compensation for the disappointment of a failed marriage Bellow would certainly welcome the attention of a biographer. But Bellow already knew the potentiality for bitterness in critics, scholars, reviewers. Even a novelist might be a villain. For example, Updike, with his book, *Bech*, pretending to be a composite of Jewish writers but being clearly, finally, a book about Bellow, breaking out uncontrollably at last in a barrage of obscenity directed at Bellow by name. "Isn't that a good sign, that [the girls] can be obscene?" a character asks. Tonic for Updike, discharging his own obscenity, envying Bellow the certainty of his achievement.

"Separated!" I gasped, as if I hadn't known, demonstrating at that moment my own untrustworthiness.

"There's no reason why you should have known," she said, a little innocently, I think, for gossip flies fast by wire and by jet. (One day in 1965 someone told me that Bellow was "very ill." I telephoned Stern in Chicago, who assured me that that was not the case. Bellow's own elusiveness encourages such rumors. Trying to hide, trying to say No gracefully, preserving other people's feelings, he might from time to time diffuse hyperbolic accounts of himself. "Of

---

1. *Henderson the Rain King.*

course, I have known for a long time that we have inherited a mad fear of being slighted or scorned, an exacerbated 'honor.'"—this is Joseph speaking in *Dangling Man*—"It is not quite the duelist's madness of a hundred years ago. But we are a people of tantrums, nevertheless; a word exchanged in a movie or in some other crowd, and we are ready to fly at one another. Only, in my opinion, our rages are deceptive; we are too ignorant and spiritually poor to know that we fall on the 'enemy' from confused motives of love and loneliness. Perhaps, also, self-contempt.")

How had all this happened? They had seemed so happy in 1966. No, said Susan, they were not happy even then, their marriage had already begun to crack. It was her first marriage, she said, and she would never marry again. The end was undramatic. Bellow simply "moved out," she said, it was time to go, the end had come, no particular explanations. Although he was a writer he was not on all occasions a man of words.

I was eager to see Susan, and her voice made me more so. Was I interested in seeing Susan or in writing a biography of her husband? Doubtful that I could do both. On the other hand it was a feat worth trying. I'd probably soon read somewhere, once I got into it, that it *had* been done, that the biographer's way to his or her subject was through the subject's spouse.

Telephoning Morton's Steak House, I caused Bellow to be paged. The lady asked me for his first name. I declined to give it, thinking I had no right to invade his privacy in a public place. When he arrived at the telephone he seemed amused that I had made a point of it. He was surprised to hear from me—he had not known I was coming to Chicago (he said; I had reason to think otherwise)—and I was cheered by his friendliness, thinking it was a good sign pointing to his still being wide open to the question raised in my letter to him July 31, from France. He asked me when he would see me. I had another appointment this evening, I said, but I could sit with him awhile now, and he invited me to do so.

A taxicab driver declined to carry me to Morton's Steak House, pointing out that it was only three blocks away. But which three blocks? I was always a stranger to Chicago, through which I had passed for years by train and car. Lately I had thought of it as Bellow's city, thinking him even a sort of booster of the city, like Ernie

Banks. But that was another misconception of mine: I had scrambled the idea of Bellow's "success" with the idea of alliance with power, with financial and police establishments. We think all big shots band together. The big shots themselves discriminate between present power and mere literature; the best that can be said for their interest in literature, as Bellow early observed, is that they have "no objections" to it. "None will be heard as long as the interests of power are not touched."[2]

The idea of Bellow's unity with the city amused him. "Yes," he said to me on the street one night, "this hideousness, it's all mine." He has described himself as "a Chicagoan out and out." On the other hand, he told Jane Howard of *Life* that he has lived two hundred places. "My second wife used to say I was medieval pure and simple. I've always been among foreigners, and never considered myself a native of anything."[3] Herzog's second wife, Madeleine, says to her husband, "You'll never get the surroundings *you* want. Those are in the twelfth century somewhere."

I hesitated to walk in the dark, for I did not know what sort of section I was in. A lady told me to take a bus. All day on a jet plane at six hundred miles per hour. Now a city bus stopping twice in three blocks. With Bellow was his son Gregory, a man in his early twenties; a graduate student, I think, at the University of Chicago, in sociology, if I am not mistaken. Bellow studied sociology at Northwestern, but when he attempted graduate work in that field at the University of Wisconsin his academic writings turned into fiction. Gregory was dressed in a dark suit and was in general a dark fellow, not in mood but in color. Black hair on the back of his hands strikingly set off his white cuffs. I felt that he resembled his father, and Bellow and Gregory discussed the question whether Bellow himself, whose hair was now purely silver, had been curly-haired when he was Gregory's age. Curly hair mattered deeply, if not to Bellow then to his creation, Joseph, central figure and narrator of Bellow's first book, *Dangling Man*. When Joseph was in his fourth year his curls were shorn by his "self-willed" aunt in defiance of his mother. "She took me to the barber and had him cut my hair after

2. "Distractions of a Fiction Writer," *The Living Novel*, ed. Granville Hicks (New York: Macmillan Co., 1957).
3. "Mr. Bellow Considers His Planet," *Life*, April 3, 1970, p. 59.

the fashion of the time, in what was called a Buster Brown. She brought the curls back in an envelope and gave them to my mother, who thereupon began to cry. I bring this up not simply to recall how the importance of my appearance was magnified in my eyes, but also because during adolescence I was to remember this in another connection.

"In a drawer of the parlor table where the family pictures were kept, there was one to which I was attracted from earliest childhood. It was a study of my grandfather, my mother's father, made shortly before his death. It showed him supporting his head on a withered fist, his streaming beard yellow, sulphurous, his eyes staring and his clothing shroudlike. I had grown up with it. And then, one day, when I was about fourteen, I happened to take it out of the drawer together with the envelope in which my curls had been preserved. Then, studying the picture, it occurred to me that this skull of my grandfather's would in time overtake me, curls, Buster Brown, and all. Still later I came to believe (and this was no longer an impression but a dogma) that the picture was a proof of my mortality. . . . This was a somber but not a frightening thought. And it had a corrective effect on my vanity."

Gregory was open, frank. I gained a sense of him as concerned, committed, mature, serene, and hopeful, although I had heard in the past that he was at odds with his father, whose books he had been unable to read. (*Henderson the Rain King* is dedicated to him. But one of my books is dedicated to my brother who has never, I think, noticed it, and who suffers fierce headaches trying to read me. "All this fucking art," says Julius Citrine to his younger brother Charlie. "I never understood the play you wrote. I went away in the second act. The movie was better, but even that had dreary parts.") When I later said to Susan that Gregory was a lovely man—that Bellow had successfully worked that relationship through—she replied, "No, Saul hasn't changed. *Gregory* has worked it through."

I mentioned to Gregory that I had met him in New York on August 23, 1961. He asked, "How did you remember?" "He didn't remember," said Bellow, "he looked it up."

This seemed to me to be the wrong moment to ask Bellow his feelings about my letter from France. I thought that when I asked him we should be alone, so that his answer might be unaffected by the possible opinions or reactions of other persons. I drank coffee with them. Gregory was telling us his feelings about media, which angered him. He thought they were "biased." He cited, as an example, the media's view of the fighting in Vietnam, where they seemed to see the conflict as "Americans" against "Communists."

Bellow's reply has characterized him for me. I have grown older with it, learning to understand it, simple as it may seem. The problem with the media, said Bellow, was not their "bias" but their "reality"—not the semantic question of loaded words or unconscious partisanship but the essential question whether they can see an event whole, in perspective, in history. To see things whole was to be, for Bellow, nothing but trouble in the years immediately before him; he was to take a difficult and unpopular position, preserving his own vision above the clamor of the hour.

My own difficulty in accepting Bellow's viewpoint may have cost me the chance to enter into a swifter, more immediate relationship with him, as biographer. Bellow was aloof from the debate over Vietnam as he had been aloof from World War II—dangling man then and later. Joseph in his flat was "insulated here from the war." A quarter of a century later Bellow still refused to be swept up, distracted. He rejected the historic moment.

As the decade advanced, and the debate over Vietnam divided the country, Bellow maintained his view of history as time, breadth, transcendent. In a letter to me he had sarcastically described "an age" as "the interval between appearances of the Sunday Times News of the Week in Review," a nice witticism which I might then have been too preoccupied to savor. He remained at his work—in Randolph Bourne's phrase, "below the battle." Bellow once expressed himself as scornful of "the writer who was interested in war, but not in the things that cause war."[4] He required neither a gun to prove his manhood nor a public forum to prove his faith: his work was his utterance. If he was somehow an erratic father he nevertheless murdered no-one's children with a gun, airplane, or other infantile device; nor, on the other hand, led a march through the street lest it lead to the same thing.

I asked Bellow if he had read the book that I had sent him—*Twentyone Twice*, my own book of Africa and early radicalism. No, he

4. In an interview in the San Francisco *Examiner*, May 15, 1966.

was saving all books of friends to read at a later date. I told him that if he had read it and not liked it he should certainly feel free to say so, but he said no, that was not the case either, he had simply not yet read it.

He asked me whether I had read Alice Linenthal's novel. She was a San Francisco woman. I had unfortunately not. Bellow said he was "tired" of the idea of freedom for women through sexual emancipation, but whether this was a fair criticism of Linenthal's book I did not know. Her former husband, Mark Linenthal, had been a friend of Bellow's. I thought they resembled one another, but when I said so Bellow became alarmed. "He's *fat*," he said. Oh no, I said, he hasn't been fat for years, and Bellow appeared relieved.

Soon Mr. Curt Johnson appeared at our table. The Bellows prepared to depart. Johnson had with him a copy of the magazine *December*, of which he was editor, bearing upon its cover a girl in a brief dress, proclaiming itself "a magazine of the arts and opinion." Bellow said he could see the art—where was the opinion?

I should have thought the editor of a Chicago magazine would have seized the moment to solicit a contribution from Bellow, but that did not occur. Johnson apart, one thing I certainly learned during the course of my inquiry into the life of Bellow was that not every Chicago writer loves every other. Poor civic pride. A most unfortunate thing, but true. I should have thought Bellow's work would be valued for itself among discriminating readers. Often, however, Bellow's popular "success" obscures the vision of people who ought to make their own distinctions. As a result, he has left behind him pain and confusion in Chicago. His crime appears to be his failure to live up to other people's expectations. People who had once thought of him as sharing with them certain working-class ideals complain that he has ceased to be a working-class writer. Some Jews expected him to be more specifically parochial in his writing, but he has failed them, too. He is criticized for being so popular; on the other hand for his difficult academic obscurantism.

To what degree has Bellow been pleasing the market? One Mudrick, a critic, speaks of "Bellow's intention," as if a critic knows. A fine writer has summed it up for me in the following way: "I'm fascinated by your working on Bellow," she writes. "Anyway, I'm not one of those who attacked Bellow; I just figured he must be speaking to what angst-ridden New York publishers identified with, and we all have to make a living. Lucky for him for speaking the right words. Ach, that sounds as if he were tailoring his writing, and I don't mean that at all. I mean I envied him the coincidence of writing about lives which turned publishers (and obviously a lot of critics and readers) on."[5]

AMONG CHICAGO LITERARY PEOPLE of my acquaintance was Richard Ellmann, whose biography of Joyce opened my mind and eyes to many aspects of the lives of writers. I telephoned Ellmann, who appeared to be pleased to hear from me. He expressed the hope that he might see me, we hadn't seen one another since—he laughingly expected me to supply the date, knowing my habit of diary-keeping. I explained that I was just in and out of Chicago, otherwise engaged. "You sound as if you're well taken care of," he said.

I avoided mentioning my mission. I did not know what terms of friendship he and Bellow might be on; I hesitated to embarrass anyone, especially myself, by bringing together parties who might be unhappy about one another's existence. I had last seen Ellmann on August 14, 1965, in Evanston—to lunch, to the beach, to dinner that night with Ellmann and his wife, Mary, and a number of other persons at a restaurant called Fanny's, where a good deal of the table talk (not by Ellmann) consisted of an attack upon Bellow for his new novel, Herzog. As literary criticism it was inferior. It was a reckless, irrelevant linking of fictional characters with real persons off the tops of their heads with their mouths full of Fanny's food. That this should occur at table with Ellmann, whose own work was so painstaking, seemed especially ironic.

Ellmann and I talked a long time on the telephone. He had recently been to Algeria to examine some literary sites linked to the life of Oscar Wilde. He asked me whether I had read the new Frost biography, and I said I had (volume 1), and I asked him whether he had seen the new movie Ulysses. We mentioned the journals of Boswell, and he laughed, seeming to remember offhand the occasion of Boswell's encounter with Thérèse, the mistress of Rousseau.

Yes, Boswell had gone to visit Rousseau, to write him up, compose a little biography, perhaps, when he received news, in Paris, of his mother's death in Scotland. He must go home. On January 31, 1766,

5. Letter from Pamela McCorduck, August 1, 1976.

therefore, Boswell, age twenty-five, set out from Paris for London in the company of Thérèse Le Vasseur, with whom, in spite of his grief at the loss of his valued mother, Boswell fornicated continually during the first eleven days of February. The pages of his journal representing those days were designated by his literary executor a "Reprehensible Passage," destroyed, and the world of course purified. However, some knowledge survived the destruction of the pages, and has been conveyed to us by the editors of the Yale Editions of the Private Papers of James Boswell:

It does not appear that before leaving Paris Boswell had formed any scheme of seducing Thérèse, and the day of his departure found him tense and harassed by difficulties in getting started, and deeply unhappy over his mother's death. But the intimacy of travel and the proximity in which the pair found themselves at inns at night precipitated an intrigue almost immediately. On the second night out they shared the same bed; Boswell's first attempt, as often with him, was a fiasco. He was deeply humiliated, the grief he was trying to repress came back upon him, and he wept. Thérèse, with a Frenchwoman's tenderness and sympathy, put her arm around him to console him and laid his hand on her shoulder. His grief and embarrassment waned; as he recorded on another occasion, his powers were excited and he felt himself vigorous. Next day he was very proud of himself, and in the coach he congratulated Thérèse (who was almost twenty years his senior) on her good fortune in having at last experienced the ardours of a Scotch lover. Thérèse stunned him by denying that she had great cause for gratitude: "I allow," she said, "that you are a hardy and vigorous lover, but you have no art." Then, with quick perception seeing him cast down, she went on, "I did not mean to hurt you. You are young, you can learn. I myself will give you your first lesson in the art of love."

He gave some details of her instruction. He must be gentle though ardent; he must not hurry. She asked him, as a man who had traveled much, if he had not noticed how many things were achieved by men's hands. He made good technical progress, though he was not wholly persuaded of her right to set up for a teacher; he said she rode him "agitated, like a bad rider galloping downhill." After a while her lectures bored him, and he brought up the subject of Rousseau, hoping at least to gather a few *dicta philosophi* for his journal. Thérèse in her turn found that dull. It was a mistake, he finally reflected, to get involved with an old man's mistress.

The first entry of the journal on the other side of the hiatus not only furnishes unequivocal evidence of the liaison, but also vindicates Boswell's claim to vigor.

WEDNESDAY 12 FEBRUARY. Yesterday morning had gone to bed very early, and had done it once: thirteen in all. Was really affectionate to her.[6]

Ellmann laughed. "Thirteen times en route," he said. "Incredible."

Such things happen.

I NEGLECTED TO MENTION to Bellow at Morton's Steak House my having spoken to Susan, and I do not think I have mentioned even *here* our arrangement to have lunch together on the following day. Other people's marital separations are a trial for me. I resist partisanship. Therefore I had tried to stress to Susan that I was in Chicago not only to see Bellow—that I should be more than pleased to see her as well—to which she encouragingly replied, alluding to our meeting of the previous year, "I liked you and I'd like to see you."

When she failed to arrive at our meeting-place I became uneasy and telephoned her at her home, quickly becoming engaged in a difficult and moving conversation with Daniel, age three, who, thinking that I was his father, repeatedly uttered a word I could not distinguish, and told me that he loved me. I could not but tell him that I loved him in turn, and I think I fooled him with my voice. Certainly I fooled the black lady who took the phone from Daniel and addressed me as "Mr. Bellow." An untrustworthy biographer! Impersonating his subject!

I remembered Daniel as a stocky boy with dark, curly hair, who, when I saw him, had impressed me with the way he flung himself onto the couch, as if he were apart from himself—a sack heaving itself. How can a father leave home? It is beyond my understanding.

6. *Boswell on the Grand Tour . . . 1765–1766*, ed. Frank Brady and Frederick A. Pottle (New York: McGraw-Hill, 1955), pp. 293–95.

How leave a child behind? Said Susan, "After the first one it's easy." Bellow had three sons—Gregory, Adam, and Daniel. I asked Susan if Gregory and Adam were full brothers. She replied, "Nobody's a full brother."

We were to meet at the northeast corner of Fifty-Third Street and Hyde Park Boulevard, but when I arrived there I was at a loss to know directions. A man said to me, "The Lake is always east." The morning had been raining, but now we had sun, and Susan appeared. Her face was mature, seasoned, and glistening like the day. She kept her eye on the time, since she had an appointment after lunch with her psychiatrist, an elderly woman. Was the treatment helpful? She could not say, she said, she could only know eventually. We discussed whether it were probable that we know all about ourselves eventually with or without medical help. Age is all. Some do, some don't, she said. Of course it was Bellow she was talking about. The "some" who "don't" was he. He would never change. She viewed him as Feffer viewed Sammler, as "a fixed point," even as I, too, had viewed Bellow, thinking of him as immobile, fixed, finished, prepared to sit still for his biography. But he was no fixed point, he was in motion, incomplete, changing. We all make mistakes. We need to be informed by friends and lovers. "Friends are harder to find than lovers," said Susan.

At lunch at the Courthouse Restaurant Susan recalled my saying in *Twentyone Twice* that my writing was my psychoanalysis. She had been reading it—Bellow had "left it behind," she said. I asked whether he had "left it behind" or *didn't intend to take it*. The distinction was unimportant to Susan, but she saw that it mattered to me. "What did he tell you?" she asked.

"That he was saving friends' books to read later," I replied.

She asked, "What friends?"

Her head ached. She had been awakened early by Daniel, and she had smoked too soon. She lamented Bellow's "neglect" of Daniel, saying that when Bellow came to visit Daniel he made promises he did not keep, that she herself could not help but weep to see Daniel's disappointment when Bellow, instead of remaining for dinner, went off into the night. Ah yes, that was the word I hadn't been able to distinguish—"dinner, dinner," that was the word Daniel was saying. "Two marriages, two children," Herzog ironically reflects, "and he was setting off for a week of *carefree* rest. It was painful to his instincts, his Jewish family feelings, that his children should be growing up without him. But what could he do about that?" A "loving but bad father"—that was Herzog.

I had not intended to rush with Susan into my idea of writing Bellow's biography. Indeed, I had not planned to tell her at all on this day. But I soon announced it—too soon, swiftly, shockingly soon, almost before we had begun our lunch. I *will* tell women things. I'd make a rotten international spy, the touch of a woman unseals me. "The thing I have in mind to do," I said, "is to write a biography of Saul."

Flatly she asked, "Why would you want to do that?"

I could not understand her question. I was a writer and I sought suitable subjects to write about. A biography of a worthy writer lies well within the tradition of literature. Then, too, I felt obliged to respect my own processes: the idea of a biography of Bellow had shaken down in my head over a long period of time. Persisted; would not go away. "Because he makes me more human," I said.

"He doesn't do that for me," she said. She said that I would be foolish to write his biography. "He'll never tell you the truth. It will all come out lies."

"Of course I'll need to *sift* things," I replied, "stay within the limits of things I can truly know. Or if I don't know something I'll make it clear I was speculating. I won't invent things. I won't say 'Women believe' if I've only heard it from one or two women. I won't make up things people say or give them fictional actions—'he said, flipping away his cigarette.'" Had she read the new biography of Frost? I wrote the name down for her, citing Frost as a man who was also hard upon wife and children, who placed his art before all other obligations.

She asked, "Do you approve that? Do you approve this cruelty to wives and children?"

No, I said, but I thought artists couldn't help themselves.

How is it more honorable, Susan argued, or less despicable, for an artist to place his art before his other obligations than for a businessman to place his *money* before other obligations? We despise the businessman for such a system of values, and yet we celebrate the artist for the same offense.

I wasn't *celebrating*, I said, I was only describing. If my biography of Bellow was nothing more than a form of celebration I'd stop it this minute. Susan's grief and anger excited me. Suppose I were forced to choose between Susan and Bellow, whom would I choose? In that moment, Susan. "Such beauty makes men breeders, studs and servants," Herzog thinks, playing his oboe, watching Madeleine drive away.

In Susan's case, I said, it was apparently true that a certain disenchantment had set in. A man is no hero to his estranged wife. Yet Bellow enchanted many other persons. I had reason to believe, for example, that Bellow was the object of the fantasies of many women everywhere. Susan asked me how I knew this. I cited the most recent example I could summon to mind, the dark and beautiful professor with whom I had dined in San Francisco only two weeks before, who either imagined herself occupying a beach house in southern California (or did) with "the whole cast of *Herzog*," including, needless to say, Herzog himself. Susan pressed for her name, but I could not remember it.

Speaking for herself, Susan said, although it may be true that Bellow occupies the fantasies or even the real beds of thousands of admiring ladies, and although he might be, as I ("you, Mark") said, a literary worker of significant rank or order in the history of American letters (on this point she was skeptical without wishing to be detained), nevertheless she thought that my writing his biography was more honor than he deserved. A biography honored a great man, and it just wouldn't occur to her to think of him as a great man, knowing him as she did. Denise scolds Charlie Citrine in the following way: "I just can't believe the way you are. The man who's had all those wonderful insights, the author of all these books, respected by scholars and intellectuals all over the world. I sometimes have to ask myself, 'Is that *my* husband? The man *I* know?'" Bellow was Susan's separated husband, that was all. It simply astonished her to discover how worthwhile I considered him, she had quite forgotten that he had ever been or could ever be again, for her or for anyone, anybody more than her recent unsatisfactory spouse. She saw him in that role only. He had never been *her* fantasy.

Never?

Slowly things came back to her. She now recalled, yes, shadowy aspects of the man she had known and married five years ago when he had in fact been (now that her mind adjusted to the memory) not only a private handsome man but a public man already famous within the realm of books—*Henderson the Rain King* and *Seize the Day* were new then, *Herzog* was on the way. He had been, in fact, come to think of it, her fantasy after all, before his descent into reality, which sheared him, reducing him to nothing more than the real, difficult, disenchanted husband of his third wife, Susan.

Unfortunately it was necessary to go; and this exactly at the moment when we were gaining intimacy on the subject of Bellow. After all, it was our shared direction, from fantasy to reality, from the dream to biography, celebration to fact. But Susan was required to keep her appointment with her psychiatrist. She drove me to a point two blocks from my hotel, and there we parted with mutual assurances that we should soon meet again to revive our conversation. As it turned out, however, at our next encounter she was guarded. She drove off through the afternoon sunshine to her psychiatrist.

I MOVED MYSELF and my baggage from the Hotel Del Prado to the Center for Continuing Education, on the Midway Plaisance, on the campus of the University of Chicago. For the past five years, I believe, Bellow had been a professor at the university, associated with something called the Committee on Social Thought, which in all journalistic biography of Bellow is described with an adjective— sometimes it is called the "prestigious" Committee on Social Thought, sometimes the "august" Committee on Social Thought. I do not know what the Committee on Social Thought is, or what it does, or whether it is prestigious or august. Maybe it is a hoax. Maybe it is a poker club.

Many adjectives may also be applied to a writer. The more favorable the adjectives the more elevated will the writer appear to reporters and readers, and the more secure everyone will be who undertakes to read or write about a writer already well-supported by adjectives. One need not then arrive at his or her own estimate or comprehension of the writer.

I have here at hand a typical college anthology whose editor writes of Bellow that he is "often acknowledged as the most distinguished American novelist of his generation." This is simply meaningless. What is "distinguished"? "Acknowledged" by whom? How often is often? The same editor tells of the "many honors awarded" Bellow, such as Guggenheim Fellowships, National Book Awards, and "the International Literature Prize." Who gives these prizes, and what do the people know who give them?

"*Herzog* accumulated prizes; a play called *The Last Analysis* did not." So says a picture caption of Bellow in *Life*. Is *Herzog* therefore a worthy book but *The Last Analysis* an unworthy play? For any individual reader or playgoer something quite different might be true. Alas! We are individually at the mercy of critics and caption-writers, whose tastes, standards, feelings, souls, interiors, may not be ours but theirs. "Prizes" may not be judgments of work but judgments of judgments, judgments of captions, judgments of other prizes. Almost no critics in a commercial *milieu* are capable of resisting prior commercial judgment: if a play has succeeded it must be good, and if it has not succeeded it must be bad. The idea of "success" is extremely slippery, and for that reason I am trying to be alert to the word I so habitually use, and to express my skepticism with quotation marks.

As for academic critics, almost none who has written about Bellow (almost none who writes about anybody) dares to begin to gather his thoughts without first strewing to the winds clusters of verification. The safest beginning is to mention *other* academic critics who are working on Bellow, figuring out all the symbols he has scattered like bread-crumbs as he goes, Hansel and Gretel in the fearful woods. Critics penetrate his philosophy, trying to translate it into known systems, tracing his sources to accepted literary or philosophical places or persons. Those are the academic equivalent of commercial achievement, although academic critics defer to commerce, too: a prize, a best-seller, mere print itself generate respect.

Commercial critics and academic critics collaborate on book jackets and in advertising to destroy the mind of a public which requires not abuse but instruction. In a shower of superlatives words cease to mean. Most, best, finest, highest, first. Fawcett advertising calls Bellow "the most intelligent novelist . . . the finest stylist" in America, but in fact it cares so little for literature that in listing Bellow's work it omits books published elsewhere than at Fawcett. (Incredibly, Avon Books, publishers of the soft-cover *Humboldt's Gift* in 1976, lists only *The* [sic] *Dangling Man* and *The Victim* as "other books by Saul Bellow.") Nathan A. Scott, Jr., says Augie March is "certainly the most memorable comic presence in recent fiction," and *Time* says that *Mr. Sammler's Planet* is "easily the most exciting" of Bellow's. Irving Howe calls Bellow the "most serious" and "the best living American novelist," and the late Harvey Swados says Bellow is "more alive" than anyone else.

But we are all equally alive until we are dead. We associate literary critics with language, but they employ it wildly, senselessly, irrationally, buried beneath considerations so tangled that the clearheaded artist, whom the world calls emotional, can only sigh. "You don't *read* such stuff," Bellow said once to me, so heatedly, so impatiently, with such disappointment in me, that I interpreted his challenge as a firm description of his own response.

I have never thought Bellow was the most or the best or the first. I do not believe he should have received *three* National Book Awards since I deplore the process at the outset. Nobody is that much better than everybody else. Happily, he fulfills his obligation to the rest of us by singling out the system for its witlessness. His good Dr. Braun "did not care much for being *first* in the field." The mentality of games pollutes us: not the thing matters, but the winning. LITERATURE GIVES U.S. NOBEL SWEEP said the headline of one newspaper which editorially compared the Nobel competition to "an Olympics of the mind." It was "an unprecedented sweep . . . a clean sweep."

One of my points of admiration for Bellow is his outspoken skepticism of the process. Writing begins as a protection for self, for feeling, for expression. In an essay critical of academic criticism, Bellow wrote, "It would take an unusual professor to realize that Achilles *was* angry."[7] A silly critic called Bellow's essay a "tirade,"[8] but it was Bellow, not the critic, who believed in the passion of literature. "Perhaps the deepest readers are those who are least sure of themselves. An even more disturbing suspicion is that they prefer meaning to feeling."[9] Critics "can't know what the imagination is nor what its powers are. I wish I could believe in their good-natured objectivity. But I can't. I should like to disregard them, but that is a little difficult because they have a great deal of power. Not real power, perhaps, but power of a sort. And they can be very distracting. But the deadly earnestness with which they lower the boom! On what? after all. On flowers. On mere flowers."[10]

7. "Deep Readers of the World, Beware!" *New York Times Book Review*, February 15, 1959.
8. "Patterns of Rebirth in *Henderson the Rain King*," *Modern Fiction Studies*, Winter 1966/67, p. 413.
9. "Deep Readers of the World, Beware!"
10. "Distractions of a Fiction Writer," pp. 6–7.

But the truest reason for my extreme admiration of Bellow is that his writings have enriched my life, personally, privately, and would have served me in that way had he never won a prize, a poll, or a superlative. The writings of many other persons have enriched my life in the same way. Bellow has always told me things I did not know. Perhaps I was on the verge of knowing them. In style, tone, he was out ahead of me, beckoning me. He was a marvel at details of face, of food, of skin, of surgery, of medicine, of flowers, of cars, of animals, of plants, of trees, of human speech, of the anatomy of men in steambaths, of streets, of automobiles, of clothing, of furniture, of obsessions, of family memory, of irate women, of men believing they are reasoning, of charlatans, of courtrooms, of street scenes, of moments I remember beyond the wholeness of the books they inhabit: the woman physician saving the life of the circumcised Polish Jew, the Chassid on the airplane offering Bellow money to be kosher, the dead birds in the toilet at Ludeyville, the battlefield of the six-day Israeli war, Mr. Sammler and the pickpocket on the bus and afterward, waterpipes bursting in the house of Dr. Gruner, Wallace Gruner's project in aerial photography, Henderson lifting Mummah clear of the ground, Cantabile and Citrine in the shithouse. On the girder. Cantabile demolishing Citrine's Mercedes with baseball bats (Citrine telephones home two unmatchable words: "Car trouble"), Julius Citrine obsessively eating, Herzog's collision leaving the aquarium, on, on, Bellow's language, formal and colloquial in the same stroke, wondrous in its timing, its infinite resourcefulness, its seeming carelessness. Madeleine studying in bed. Renata masturbating with Citrine's foot under the Plaza table—then stealing his shoe. I rejoice in his hyperbole, his vision. I surrender myself to his style, try to imitate it, and so improve my own, and all these valuable things Bellow has done for *me*.

For you he might do nothing.

Bellow as person was troublesome, however. This is why biographers prefer dead subjects. From my point of view he was difficult to deal with. He was witty, charming, and irritable. He scolds. He criticizes freely. He has raised my consciousness and given me enormously useful advice about writing and living.

Fortune and reputation made him prey of several persons and various forms of exploitation. Various people were into him. For something. Maybe he thought I was into him, too. Maybe I was—

"swindled, conned, manipulated, his savings taken, driven into debt, his trust betrayed by wife, friend, physician"—poor Herzog. And poor Herzog after *Herzog*, when the money advanced geometrically!

Exploited yes, but deceived no. That part of me that was flesh he may have doubted, but that part of me which was paper he could read, and he assisted me in several ways, especially by preserving in print work of mine which would otherwise have died upon the shelf, and a part of me with it. Wrong to say, as someone said in a magazine, that Bellow is a great artist but a bad friend. Like Frost, he teaches by thorniness.

IN THE Center for Continuing Education I was the only guest in a building of one hundred and seventeen rooms. The most recent conference had departed; mine had not assembled.

About five o'clock Dick Stern came for me. Stern as writer is quite as committed as Bellow, not less exciting, not less intelligent, not less distinctive in his style, less available than Bellow to a popular reading audience. He is the author of seven novels, other fiction, and superior reportage, much of it awaiting the appreciation of time. He is difficult reading for many people. When I first met him, in 1961, he gave me a play in manuscript. I thought it good and lively and profound. The writer Philip Roth recommended it to a Broadway producer, Max Gordon, who had told Roth, "Even if it only looks like a play George Kaufman can make a play out of it." But after awhile came a second message from Gordon to Roth: "I read your professor's play but even George Kaufman couldn't make a play out of it." Such is the gulf between one kind of mind and another. Bellow, too, was frustrated by Broadway.

Bellow as best-seller may be a trick of sociology. I cannot otherwise explain it. People expect from his books the wrong kind of joy. Booksellers have told me that he sells very fast to a disappointed public. I have been a lucky beneficiary—I buy many Bellow books secondhand soon after publication. Once I received a copy free: I was sitting on an airplane beside a man reading *Herzog*. When I asked him if he were enjoying it he said he must be, since it was on the best-seller list, but soon he slapped it angrily into my lap. "*Have* it," he said.

Stern and Bellow met in 1957. They have shared the same neighborhood, the same employer, offering each other criticism and counsel in their trials and dilemmas. Stern is a friend of Bellow's stable side, sober, reliable, immensely learned, though not without eccentricities of mind and physique which I seem to see distributed in Bellow's fiction. When I met him he and his wife, Gay, had three "talented and placid" children, says my diary—it was a part of my youth and innocence to think "placid" was good—and Gay was pregnant with their fourth child. Speaking of marriage, Stern once attributed Bellow's difficulties in that field to his marrying "vaguely intellectual" women. Thus the marriages "came apart." Said Stern: "His relationships lack glue. He *admires* glue, but he doesn't have it himself. You and I are men of glue." Years later, however, Stern's own marriage "came apart." His novel, *Other Men's Daughters*, strikes me as perhaps drawing upon that experience.

I thought Stern was undoubtedly my best advisor in the matter of Bellow's biography. Therefore, when he arrived at the Center for Continuing Education I promptly told him my idea. His response was everything I could have hoped for. *Enthusiast*—that's a top-notch word for Dick, to go with *bolsterer*. I in turn was deeply relieved to hear his enthusiasm, both for my idea itself, and upon the grounds that Stern was entitled by long and faithful friendship to prior rights, so to speak. If he had any plans along that line I would step aside. Perhaps with relief.

"No," he said, "it never entered my mind. Recently, when Saul went off on an airplane somewhere I thought, 'If he goes down I'll have to write a piece.'" But biography had never entered his mind. "I'm too close to him," he said. "It's funny he didn't mention receiving your letter."

"I thought it was funny myself."

"It's nothing to *worry* about," said Stern.

"Maybe he didn't want to discuss it," I said.

"Not with me," said Stern.

"Not with anybody," I said. "Maybe he dismissed it from his mind right away."

"No," said Dick, "he'd be flattered that you want to do it."

Of course I was encouraged by his remarks. He said it was particularly appropriate that a novelist should undertake such a work, for a novelist is notable "not only because he invents but because of the way he *arranges* material."

"I won't be *inventing*," I defensively said. "But it's true I'll be arranging."

"Of course," he said, impatient to see the work begun, as if I could start that very minute. "Why didn't you mention this to him last night?"

"His son was there."

"Oh, for Christ's sake," said Stern, "the kid's only three years old."

"No, Gregory," I said. "Not Daniel."

"Never mind who's there," said Stern, "mention it to him tonight."

He was eager to get going. Avanti with Vita Bellorum. In his '63 Chrysler we set out. Stern is a large man, tall and sturdy. To some extent he lumbers, rolls, or sways as he walks. He has bulk, and a gaze of distraction optical and cerebral, laughing into space, a well-functioning citizen, open, responsible, capable of useful motion within society in spite of ideas probably too exotic for neighborhood civic action. I saw in him the harried character of Tommy Wilhelm: "Forgetfully, Wilhelm traveled for miles in second gear; he was seldom in the right lane and he neither gave signals nor watched for lights. . . . He dreamed at the wheel or argued and gestured, and therefore the old doctor would not ride with him." In this passage from *Herzog*, too, I see Stern: "Mornings he tried to reserve for brainwork. He corresponded with the Widener Library to try to get the *Abhandlungen der Königlich Sächsischen Gesellschaft der Wissenschaft*. His desk was covered with unpaid bills, unanswered letters. To raise money, he took on hackwork. University presses sent manuscripts for his professional judgment. They lay in bundles, unopened." In those days his fingertips were dry, and he ran them often like scales on his tongue.

His concentration was intense. Once it saved his child's life. In his big house one day, while he was writing, a drug-addict held one of his children at knife-point, instructing Gay to find money in the house. She said she must go to her husband. But not one word, said the assailant. Entering Stern's study, Gay held out her open hand. Luckily, silently, never taking his eye from his work, Stern withdrew his wallet from his pocket and passed it to her.

"Your biography of Bellow will be *unprecedented*," Stern said.

"Somebody was saying," I said, "that he doesn't always tell the truth."

"He's as big as his books," Dick said. "He's not afraid of petty revelations." (Bellow said to me some time afterward: "What can you reveal about me that I haven't already revealed about myself?")

Stern had recently read *Twentyone Twice*, which was now in Susan's possession. Stern said that my "persona" in that book was "innocence," that I as a person really knew a great deal more about life than I revealed in print.

"Very perceptive," I said. "I'm not exactly what I say I am in the book. I make myself innocent to protect others. If I'm a person who understands too much I might tell too much. That's how I think I've got to do the Bellow biography: oblique, glancing, not knowing too much."

Stern now seemed to be having some second thoughts. "He'll always be self-conscious in the presence of the biographer," he said.

"I'll have to come to Chicago an awful lot," I said.

"He'll never be able to be completely himself when you're around."

I saw myself coming to Chicago in different seasons of the year, in the snow, in the heat, sloshing through the sleet with Bellow, seeing life over his shoulder.

"I'm wondering about that," said Stern.

"It will be a spectacular education for me," I said.

"His life will be different," Stern said. "He requires privacy."

"Think of my burden," I said, "trying to get it all down. That's the worst strain, keeping it organized, and yet pursuing at the same time, digging, opening new directions, probing. And then, when the fun is over, I'm the one who's got to go home and write it. I'll be glad when it's done."

"Years and years," said Stern. "Are you sure?"

"Maybe ten or fifteen years," I guessed. From that day to the day I began actually to compose was nine years and two months. Not a bad guess! "But listen," I asked, "suppose he says No."

"He won't say No," said Dick.

We arrived at the Sterns' house at 4901 South Kimbark. There we were to meet Bellow. That was the plan. The Sterns' house was spacious. I admired especially the splendid wood paneling. I again met Gay, reminding her that she had been pregnant when I last saw her on April 6, 1961. "Not pregnant now," she said with satisfaction. Their four children one by one came forward from various rooms of the house; and a child or children of Gay's sister, who was visiting.

A message awaited Dick from Bellow, who was this very hour,

Dick said, in the company of his *bonne amie*. Stern spoke in slightly evasive language in the presence of the children. But Bellow was on the way, Dick said.

Soon, however, Bellow telephoned again to say that he had lost his wallet and intended to return to his home to see if he had left it there. He had been all day at his lawyer's, Dick said, perhaps in connection with his taxes. He had recently made a tax payment of forty thousand dollars, mainly against revenue from *Herzog*, and as a further defense against taxes he had given his house at Tivoli as a gift outright to Bard College. The manuscript he had read to me in that house with his hat on had cost him the house itself. "The government, which had taken no previous interest in my soul," Charlie Citrine complains, "immediately claimed seventy percent in the result of its creative efforts."

Citrine laments that he had "bungled the whole money thing." Yes, bungled it because he had never thought about it, never prepared for it, never expected it. Visions of sugar plums had never been Bellow's, apart from anything in the head of Thomas Meehan in *The New Yorker* over the Atlantic Ocean. Bastards of the government, bastards at law tried to devour Bellow. "Oh! the might of money and the entanglement of art with it—the dollar as the soul's husband: a marriage nobody has had the curiosity to study." Accountants were into him, judges were into him, wives were into him. Citrine "owed publishers about seventy thousand dollars in advances for books I was too paralyzed to write. I had lost interest in them utterly."

Bellow knew nothing of bag men, of secret numbered accounts in foreign banks, of laundered money. Those things were the devices of patriots: President Nixon, for example. The little tragedy was not the money. The tragedy was as Citrine said—that neither the government nor its people was much interested in anything until the money entered. For Citrine it was education finally: "But I was beginning to see the American dollar-drive for what it was. It had assumed the proportions of a cosmic force. It stood between us and the real forces."

I heard that Bellow telephoned the Sterns' house four or five times a day. Susan Bellow said that such a steady ringing must be agony for Gay. "Saul is on the loose," said Susan, "dragging Dick through the streets at all hours of the night." For a few minutes now we all sat in the living-room—the Sterns, Gay's sister, and the children, among them Andrew Stern, sixteen, a great tall child with a basket-ball in his arms. Soon he left, and then Gay's sister, and then Gay, too, saying she and her sister had much visiting to do in the kitchen, leaving Stern and me finally somewhat awkwardly sitting at an in-hospitable distance from one another.

Gay's complexion was slightly red, as if she had some sort of rash upon her cheeks. Her leaving the room made me think of her as in-different, uninterested, cool until once when, in a moment of happi-ness I took her hand, it was deliciously and surprisingly warm, and I could guess that her life was plentiful, but in another room.

Again Bellow telephoned, this time to announce that he had found his wallet. We agreed to go to his apartment instead of his coming to the Sterns'. Therefore we went. I do not know where. I do not know how long we drove to reach there, so intensely were Stern and I talking. It was evening, dark.

Bellow's apartment was small, somewhat cramped, and in its character not at all his. Later that year he moved to a grander apart-ment. Maybe this was a borrowed apartment. I was introduced to his companion, Bonne Amie, a woman who instantly charmed me in a number of ways, not the least of which was her telling me that her mother-in-law admired my work. Afterward, however, in Lafayette, Indiana, where I became associated with Purdue University, her mother-in-law attacked me in the newspaper for my activities against the Vietnam war, declaring that I was a leader of a lawless mob pledged to burn down Purdue.

Bonne Amie was slightly dark, as if Latin, and she wore trans-parent net stockings upon legs slightly plump which she crossed in a graceful way. She was the mother of two children. She had come to town from Iowa City, where she was to receive a master's degree in creative writing. What better way to study creative writing than by attaching herself to Bellow? Education is just hangin' around, said Frost. She may have been one of those "vaguely intellectual" women to whom Stern referred, but that may not be different from her being one who harbored that "sealed treasure" Bellow knew in the souls of women. She readily laughed, but I think she was some-times uncertain why. Laughing on faith. Laugh now, comprehend later.

"Go ahead," said Stern to me, "mention this other matter."

I should broach my biographical idea! "Now?"

"Open the discussion," said Stern.

I remember that we were standing, leaving. We had never removed our coats. We must have been waiting for Bonne Amie to return from another room. "No, this isn't the time," I said, but Stern insisted that it *was* the time, and I reflected to myself that Stern knew Bellow a thousandfold better than I, and if Stern said it was the time it was, and I should be well-advised to do as he said. Else why had I gone to Stern in the first place? I said to Bellow, "By the way, regarding my letter."

He was perplexed, or appeared so. He said, "What letter was that, Mark?"

I was chilled. "Of July thirty-first of last year," I said. He was in no way enlightened. "My letter from France," I said, "where I asked you if I might write your biography?"

He looked at neither Stern nor me, staring off between our heads, his face whitening as he drew to himself either the idea for the first time, or his renewed resistance to it. Nothing in his face revealed either that he favored my idea or opposed it, or even that he heard it. He searched his mind for the letter, not for his response, saying so inaudibly he must have been speaking to himself, "I didn't receive any letter." He sat upon a chair (one chair, later, was all I could remember of the furnishings of that apartment), still staring straight forward, not at me, not at Stern—"He won't say No," Stern had said, and indeed Bellow said neither No nor Yes nor anything further but simply kept his silence, permitting the idea to move out, even as he had moved out, Susan said, undramatically, no particular explanations, as if now by the invisible power of his impassivity my idea would rise like an odor into the pores of the ceiling, or like a *faux pas* escape notice if we pretended not to have heard it.

Chapter Three

WHERE WAS I? Who were we who were now leaving Bellow's little apartment? Was I the biographer and Bellow my subject? Should I ask him again—maybe he hadn't heard me? After we had reached the street Bellow went back to his apartment. I imagined in that moment that he had returned to attend to something related to my appeal. But that now appears absurd to me. I invested the moment with an importance beyond reality. Yet maybe not. Half a year later I had reason to believe he thought I was *telling*, not asking, that I was simply informing him that I was intending to "do" him anyhow, whether he liked it or not. Such a thing had never occurred to me, but since I had a *legal* right to do so, and even in the free-speech sense a *moral* right—and since he was in those days caught up in courtrooms and judges' chambers where people pressed their legal rights apart from persons or feelings—he may have imagined my suing him for nothing less than my right to be his biographer apart from his willingness. It was a year of non-negotiable demands, rising expectations.

Maybe he had returned to his apartment for his hat, because in Stern's '63 Chrysler, when I looked back at Bellow, he was wearing a little porkpie hat pulled forward over his eyes, looking out from under his brows, smiling back and forth with Bonne Amie in a private and joyful way. With his hat pulled down and his coat buttoned high he gave me the impression of having very little face. His teeth shone and his eyes danced, but the reason for his good spirit was unclear to me. Perhaps he was anticipating the night beyond the evening, for

43

this was a reunion, I believe, with Bonne Amie. He seemed to have forgotten all about my biography.

Stern, as we drove, was once more overcome by a vision of tragedy, saying that in the event of an automobile mishap "this would be quite a literary loss." Here was superstition reversed, a way of defying Fate by daringly announcing the option. Bellow said that on a recent airplane flight one of his fellow passengers was Robert Graves: Bellow had felt that if the plane went down he (Bellow) would go down at least in distinguished company. Fresh from my disappointment in Bellow's apartment, I now took an antiliterary position. Who cares for literary men or women? Who cares if four writers crash on the streets of Chicago. I took the ultra-democratic human-love position that any four persons in a car-pool home from the factories are as important to themselves and to their families and *to the world* as any four writers.

Bellow, too, appeared to be involved in some sort of correction, sending forth suggestions of snobbism to counteract my democracy. Although he and Stern had agreed upon the restaurant, Bellow, when we arrived, took me aside, saying, "This is *Stern's* choice of a restaurant." As if the style of the restaurant were pitched at the wrong level for *Bellow*. A biographer should be clear about this! Nor should a biographer be disappointed, lose respect for his subject. The author of fine work is a man of taste in restaurants.

Worst of all, henceforth I was destined for a time to behave in Bellow's presence not better than I really was, but worse. My moment of democracy gave way. He brought out that side of me which preferred (or thought that Bellow would prefer) to stress or advertise my active hustle, my athleticism, my being not of the world of meditation or reflection, but of the world of "success." I would be proving something to Bellow, showing off, losing ground, shooting up and down the general area west of the Rockies.

The restaurant was decent, I thought, but Bellow had once been served a poor steak here, and he was unforgiving. As we took our places at table we were greeted by a young, slightly effeminate, rather nervous man, described to me afterward as an accomplished musician, who indicated his desire to sit with us awhile (he had already eaten), but who soon became the target of some joshing remarks of Bellow's. This delicate fellow sat a moment, measured the strain, and withdrew, routed. Bellow's mood had changed from the joy of the back of the automobile to a sort of irritation. Perhaps his blood-sugar level was down. When the musician disappeared he chided Stern once more, as a *nouveau-riche*.

Two significant incidents occurred.

First, I was unable to mention having had lunch with Susan. (The night before, at Morton's Steak House, I had been unable to mention making my appointment with her.) Had I been acknowledged Bellow's biographer I should have been guiltless, and mentioned it. Or had I never applied to be Bellow's biographer! But having applied and been (or so I felt) repulsed, my having had lunch with Susan now appeared to me to have been exactly the sort of thing Bellow suspected me of being capable of: of prying, meddling, that old journalistic vulturism, swooping down precisely on that person who was most vulnerable, most hurt, defenseless, who might therefore have the most urgent reason to surrender to the world of gossip the least flattering secrets of her recent husband.

Quite apart from filching immaterial secrets, I was threatening to appropriate objects of utmost reality—lives themselves—one moment dining with Susan as man and woman, another moment breathing endearment to Daniel on the telephone. Moving in. "She doesn't run around with men," Aunt Zelda told Herzog. "They phone her all the time, chasing after her. Well—she is a beauty, and a very rare type, too, because she is so brilliant. Down there in Hyde Park—as soon as everybody knew about the divorce, you'd be surprised who all started to call her." When Herzog's lawyer, Sandor Himmelstein, took Madeleine "to lunch at Fritzl's . . . guys who haven't given Sandor H. the time of day for years came running with a hard-on, tripping over themselves. That includes the rabbi of my temple. She's some dish." Behavior of that kind was no news to Bellow, but it placed me in the category of everyman at a moment when I wished to be thought of as someone higher, nobler, his most discreet, fastidious, trustworthy, impeccable, confidential, close-mouthed biographer.

Bellow was altering me. My character shifted. The longer I delayed mentioning my lunch (luncheon, really) with Susan the more the whole event appeared to have been a hostile calculation from the beginning. I delayed so long mentioning my luncheon with Susan that the possibility dissolved—if not a calculation why mention it now?—one *begins* with small talk. Of what was I guilty? Was it sexual play? But a man who thought sexual play worried Bellow was hardly the man to be his biographer. ("You ain't getting no maiden," said Leo Durocher to *his* biographer.) Within a few minutes, without having moved from my place at table, I had become both guilty of having had lunch or luncheon with Susan, and of not having mentioned it; and the longer I took to mention it the more sinister the lunch itself became in my mind, even though it had been a very innocent luncheon (perhaps).

All evening long my Freudian tongue was unable to avoid it. I had occasion to begin several sentences in a manner habitual with me, "Someone was saying at lunch today . . ." Suppose Bellow, Stern, or Bonne Amie were to ask me who had said it, or where. Well, I was unable to remember the name of the restaurant. Natural enough. I was a stranger in the city. But surely—Bellow speaking, let us say— you can remember, if not the name of the restaurant, the name of the person. Distracted, I rehearsed a little story. I had lunch at a forgotten restaurant with—perhaps the dark and beautiful professor from San Francisco State (doing what in Chicago in March?) whose name had come up between Susan and me. But her name had precisely *not* come up. I had *forgotten* her name, though Susan pressed for it, nor had I reclaimed it by dinner-time in a restaurant whose name I never knew, or forgot.

And I forget it now.

The second significant incident was this: as we were settling the bill Bellow referred to *himself*, as he had earlier baited Stern, as *nouveau-riche*. It was an apology to Stern, and I thought it was gracious and fine. But now I once again felt compelled to set myself apart, as I had done in the car on the question of vehicular mishap. In a tentative, fumbling way, rehearsing a new little playlet—improvising, my story-making mechanism rooting for details to support the climax I intended—I insisted that we were all, after all, quite rich, that our incomes were in the upper one percent of mankind taken whole, as I had recently seen in a chart in a magazine.

Moreover, not *nouveau-riche*, either, but reasonably established as rich, knowing the feeling of money. "Feffer had a strange need to cover himself with the brocade of boasts. Money, brag—Jewish foibles. American too?" My tale expanded. Notice embedded in my narrative facts which of themselves improve my standing, raising me toward equality with Bellow: for example, the fact that my first novel was published in 1946, only two years after Bellow's first novel, *in spite of his being seven years older than I.*

"When my first novel was published," I said, "in 1946 . . . or, I should say, when I received an advance for it in 1944 . . . five hundred dollars [Bellow would have said "bucks," but my very point was my elevated ease] . . . actually only four hundred and fifty after my agent's commission . . . I invested it on my father's advice in a very safe little portfolio and never touched it . . . never had any need to . . . just left it there . . . twenty-three years now . . . and just the other day when I happened to look at the little numbers I noticed that it's grown to sixty thousand dollars."

Stern gasped. "To what?"

"Introduce me to your father," said Bellow.

Where was this getting me? Bellow was the only person to whom I seemed to relate in this way. For years my admiration for him had been open and guileless, but my plan to write his biography seemed to have the effect of expanding my capacity for lying, for tampering with myself in search of an impression to please him. Worst of all, not knowing how, which only suggested my distance from his truest mind. I never lied to Robert Frost. (I never even lied to a credit house.)

My little falsehood was making me nervous, and I began to consider how to retract it or modify it. At the least, I thought with a certain panic, I damn well better find a way to freeze those funds: suppose, for example, Bellow or Stern should wish to borrow a sum of money from me, knowing how well-fixed I was! How could I, with all those "little numbers" in my portfolio, refuse my good friends? Bellow suddenly broke! In need! The government into him for seventy percent! Publishers into him! His potential biographer, whose declarations of affection are well known, has a few bucks put away. Also well known. Three witnesses in the doorway of the restaurant.

As my mind had campaigned for luncheon companions it now invented financial commitments. "Never touched it, true . . . and it's fairly well tied up for the moment . . . committed, sad to say . . . my mother . . . disabled . . ." Mercifully the matter ended in the street a few steps from the restaurant, but I have sweated out some bad thoughts of it since.

STERN DROVE endlessly, pointlessly. We must have had a destination, since eventually we arrived somewhere. But the streets of Chicago had no meaning for me except through literature. It was James T. Farrell's Chicago, Nelson Algren's, Willard Motley's, Richard Wright's, Dreiser's. Two years earlier, at Bellow's request, I had written a preface to a modern edition of Henry Blake Fuller's *With the Procession*, for a series published by the University of Chicago Press. I knew the place, but not the streets. I had grown up in it without having been there. We talked about various writers.

I mentioned Jack Conroy, who had reviewed my early work in the Chicago newspapers and made me feel like a writer, encouraging me, as he had encouraged many other young writers. I wanted to be a little careful here, for Conroy had been one of the proletarian writers of the 1930s, close to the Communists, and I wanted Bellow to understand that Conroy was somewhat at a distance from my present emotional or political state. Bellow's politics was unclear to me. I did not then know where he stood. It was not to his biographer's interest to offend him.

Bellow asked me what had happened to Conroy. I said he had retired to Moberly, Missouri. Bellow had a hard time understanding a writer's *retiring*. Retiring, I said, only from the encyclopedia for which he had worked for many years, discovering at the end that he had never really had any retirement benefits. Conroy was an easy target of economic exploitation; like Bellow, he was a lot of things before he was a shrewd moneyman; and of course, I said—as casually as I could—he had had a hard time holding a job at all throughout the McCarthy period, close to the Communists and all, maybe a Communist for all I knew, I'd really loved Jack Conroy when I was very young and had only the fondest memory of him now.

Joseph, in *Dangling Man*, had been a Communist at seventeen. He soon became disillusioned with his comrades. "By the time I got out, I realized that any hospital nurse did more with one bedpan for *le genre humain* than they did with their entire organization." I had had the idea over the years of Bellow's alignment with people whose anti-Communism was their whole politics. I early associated him, for example, with *Partisan Review*. Later I realized that his politics was loosely related, if at all, to the magazines that published him. The world wants answers, Yes or No, Left or Right. But Joseph's objection to Communist discipline was exactly that—that it demanded of him a fixed position and an end to discourse. "No, really, listen to me. Forbid one man to talk to another, forbid him to com-

municate with someone else, and you've forbidden him to think, because, as a great many writers will tell you, thought is a kind of
communication."

Bellow's humanity broadened beyond doctrine. A novelist free-
ranging sees people and the consequences of their actions as too di-
verse for systems and programs: the novelist then ends not with a
theory but with awe. The slogan of the party is "life." "Let the enemies of life step down," says Herzog, who when we first meet him
slices his bread from a loaf the rats have been into. "He could share
with rats, too." Not *kill* the enemies of life, just let them step down.
A weaponless politics even in a world where weapons appear to be
all. "One can only guess and one can only wonder," Bellow reflects
at the height of his maturity, "how all this killing is registered by
the mind and spirit of the human race. It has been estimated that
the Khmer Rouge have destroyed hundreds of thousands of Cambo-
dians as part of a design for renewal. What is the meaning of such
corpse-making? In ancient times the walls of captured cities in the
Middle East were hung with the skins of the vanquished. That
custom has died out. But the eagerness to kill for political ends is as
keen now as it ever was."[1]

To *create*, as in a good book, to make joy, laughter, design, plot, is
itself politics. "The noble will have its turn in the world," speaks
King Dahfu, and Henderson is "thrilled." One critic speaks of Bellow's "hedged affirmation." How "hedged"? If the world is not
pretty, neither is it dead. Bellow's politics is the politics of affirmation if it is politics at all. "Awareness was his work; extended consciousness was his line, his business. Vigilance."[2] Bellow won my
vote with his speech at the window at Tivoli: one sentence, and
even that a question—"Why should somebody die because I'm nervous?" But it was years before I understood that that was politics,
and in the car with him and Bonne Amie and Stern I still was wary
and uncertain. Not for some time yet would I understand that I need
not have hidden.

Fourteen months earlier, when I had seen Bellow, he had been
writing a novel inspired, as I understood it, by memories of writers
he had known. One of those writers may have been Oscar Tarcov.

1. "Reflections," *The New Yorker*, July 19, 1976, p. 80.
2. *Herzog*.

Bellow said he had thrown the manuscript away. He should not have thrown it away, I said, but should have sent it to Howard Gotlieb, at Mugar Library at Boston University, a lovely man who collects and preserves every sort of document from writers. "This summer," said Bellow, "I'll sit on the beach and send Gotlieb my sunburn peel." As we drove, his eye bounced off signs, he played on words; often he gave a more exact or accurate name to the thing he observed: he called a synagogue a "synagogo," a travel agency a "travail agency." (At dinner, hearing someone order *kirsch*, he could not help but speak of "the kirsch of an aching heart"—a melody which also danced in Herzog's head one evening on his way to visit Ramona.)

We saw a sign advertising Imperial or International Bakery. Bellow said that his father had worked for that bakery; an uncle still did. Charlie Citrine's father "slaved in the bakery." He apologized for "the historical tone" he may have taken about himself. "I don't mean to refer to myself as if I'm a historical monument, like Ellison." Bellow had shared the house at Tivoli with Ellison.

I had worked with Ellison on the Carnegie Commission during those months when I was shooting up and down the general area west of the Rockies. "I found him rude to waiters," I said. "He made me feel like a social inferior. He sure talked guns and hunting with the rich men on the commission. I felt that I was ineligible for his club."

"The gun symbolized escape from slavery," said Bellow. "He accused me of tearing up his rose bush at Tivoli. Now if I wanted to destroy his rose bush would I have *torn* it up and cut my hands with thistles? Why would I want to destroy his rose bush?"

"Rude to waiters and rude to me in Boston," I said.

"He's working on a novel of two or three thousand pages," said Bellow.

Ralph Ellison, of course, had published a single novel, *Invisible Man*, which had found a high place in American letters. I had never been able to read it—ten pages in; twenty; stopped cold, though I tried. Reviewing it in *Commentary* at the time of its publication Bellow praised its "maturity," saying "one is accustomed to expect excellent novels about boys, but a modern novel about men is exceedingly rare." Ellison's "immensely moving novel" proved "that a truly heroic quality can exist among our contemporaries."[3] As a

3. June 1952, p. 608.

novelist, however, Ellison never went forward. *Invisible Man* was atomized into a thousand anthological selections, and Ellison became a man of letters, teaching, lecturing, writing on various subjects, either wise enough to know his limits in that form, or sadly playing it safe, for no novel of his could escape comparison with *Invisible Man*.

Somehow Ellison made me think of Baldwin. Bellow had known Baldwin in Paris about 1948, 1949. In Paris, said Bellow, Baldwin seemed to insist it was necessary to be a Negro to write well. More recently he seemed to insist that in order to write well one must be a Negro *homosexual*. "But where I begin to draw the line," said Bellow, "is when Baldwin says I must be a Negro homosexual in order *to make love well to a woman*."

I asked if we were anywhere near that part of the city associated with Nelson Algren. After a brief dispute my companions seemed to agree that we were "a few blocks away." "This is where the Jews and the Irish moved to get away from the Negroes," Bellow said. Or perhaps he said "Poles," not "Irish." He offered this factually, without opinion, in the same tentative manner I had raised the name of Jack Conroy.

Algren was one of those Chicago writers who translated his own disappointment into attacks upon Bellow. In the late 1930s, Bellow has written, "I was once told by Nelson Algren, 'Some [writers] teach school; some would rather run a poker game.'"[4] If Ellison had been wise enough to withdraw from the psychic perils of the life of a novelist, Algren had made the mistake of crashing into the system. He was not the poker player he thought he was. But it was American life, not Bellow, which had tricked him—American life quite as ruthless as Algren had said it was. Where now were all the flatterers of Algren's youth, all the editors and publicists and hustlers who loved him so well when he was a hot literary property? A few years ago, when I inquired of Bellow where Algren was, he replied in a letter, "Now and then I see him around. He suffers greatly from neglect: the media no longer take pictures of him in his leather jacket as Chicago's writer. That kind of thing hurts."

Soon we were somewhere. God knew where. Bonne Amie alighted from the car, walked down an alleyway between two houses, and disappeared. Why had she gone there? Stern looked at

4. "The University as Villain," *The Nation*, November 16, 1957, p. 361.

Bellow, Bellow looked at Stern, neither knew. The motor ran, the cabin of the car became overheated, and I said that if we three died of carbon-monoxide poisoning it would be a definite literary loss. Bellow said, "She'll have to write a piece."

She did not return for a long while. Bellow said, "That's not right of her," and we speculated that some harm might have come to her down the alley, all flinging open our doors and walking quickly down the narrow alleyway in search of Bonne Amie, just as she appeared, dangling in her hand keys she had gone to fetch. She had encountered some friends, she said, and could not rudely rush right off.

AT THE STERNS' HOUSE we drank a liqueur beside the fireplace. Gay Stern sat with us awhile, and then withdrew to continue visiting with her sister. Yet she must have returned, for my notes record her being amused by the word "languished" in the passage below, which her husband read aloud. Boswell is telling of Johnson's final moments:

> Having, as has been already mentioned, made his will on the 8th and 9th of December, and settled all his worldly affairs, he languished till Monday, the 13th of that month, when he expired, about seven o'clock in the evening, with so little apparent pain that his attendants hardly perceived when his dissolution took place.[5]

Stern fired the logs, but he neglected to attend them. I speculated to myself that Gay Stern declined to sit long in our company out of loyalty to Susan Bellow. After Johnson's death she returned to her sister. Stern was for some reason reminded of the passage where Johnson says that the prospect of execution wonderfully focuses the mind (something like that). I seized the *Life* from him, saying that I could instantly find the passage. Stern waited tolerantly, I failed, and he found it easily and read:

> Johnson disapproved of Dr. Dodd's leaving the world persuaded that *The Convict's Address to his unhappy Brethren* was of his own writing. "But, Sir, (said I,) you contributed to the deception; for when Mr. Seward expressed a doubt to you that it

5. *Boswell's Life of Johnson* (London: Oxford University Press, 1953), p. 1392.

was not Dodd's own, because it had a great deal more force of mind in it than any thing known to be his, you answered,— 'Why should you think so? Depend upon it, Sir, when a man knows he is to be hanged in a fortnight, it concentrates his mind wonderfully.'"[6]

Stern was amused and laughed heartily, repeating two or three times the triumphant phrase, "concentrates his mind wonderfully." We read aloud here and there in the *Life.*

Two points about Boswell and Johnson interested Bellow especially, perhaps because of the manner in which they illuminated his own life. First, Bellow said that he thought himself impure by contrast to Johnson's "purity." I said I doubted Johnson's "purity" in the first place. True, he spoke in his will of his polluted soul ("I bequeath to God a soul polluted with many sins"), but that was more or less ritualistic. Yes, Bellow agreed, standard stuff, "everybody had soul pollution." Further, I asked, how could a "pure" man have tolerated Boswell? Johnson knew of Boswell's gambling, drinking, breaking the Sabbath, running the streets, seducing other men's wives.

Stern supported me, arguing for Johnson's perversity, citing the rumor that Johnson had engaged in flagellation. I speculated that Boswell knew of such things, too, but kept them from the record; and he was too much in awe of Johnson to believe in his sinfulness to begin with: young men think they have invented sin themselves.

Bellow's second point referred to Boswell's "melancholy." I had said I could not understand why the publication of the *Life of Johnson*, in every way so successful, brought Boswell no joy. Bellow replied to this in an interesting way which, for me at least, illuminated Bellow ever afterward: Bellow was not at all surprised, he said, that Boswell was joyless after publication of the *Life*, years and years of labor on that book had been a "crutch" for Boswell. Now the crutch was pulled out from under him. The fame of the *Life* was anticlimactic.

I interpreted Bellow as saying that Boswell's spirit died when his work was done because his subject was dead. Bellow recognized the danger of *finishing*, of polishing too bright, too fine, of rounding things off too well, sewing up every last thread.

6. Ibid., p. 849.

Bellow removed his shoes and sat in his stockinged feet. It seems to me that his fictional people are often removing their shoes. Of course, Renata at the Plaza removed *Charlie's* shoe. That was different. A special case. But love and shoes go together. In the first love affair of all, when Joseph goes to Kitty in *Dangling Man*, from his flat to her rooming house (neither place the Plaza), shy, guilty, rationalizing all the way ("Iva and I had not been getting along well"), endlessly talking, piously explaining, "amiable . . . continually smiling . . . Until, one wet and prematurely cold evening in early fall, I came in to find her in bed, drinking rum and tea." The blood "charged" to his face. His shoes stain the rug; he offers to pay for rug-cleaning. Kitty tells him to remove his wet shoes. Bending to untie his shoes, his head is "gorged" with blood.

Shoes cause it all. Sammler's daughter Shula bakes her father's shoes on the door of the oven, drying them out—"the toes were smoking." (Wallace has flooded the house seeking his father's hidden money in the water pipes.) Ramona urges Herzog to remove his shoes. "I think I will. They're already unlaced." Time after time, shoes. If Johnson was a flagellant, possibly Bellow was a shoe-fetishist. (Sammler's distant relative, Bruch, is an *arm*-fetishist, falling in love with women's arms, especially in the summer.)

In physique, Bellow is a short, slender man, perhaps weighing at that time one hundred and forty pounds. In photographs he sometimes appears taller than he is. Perhaps he arranges it that way— perhaps has that vanity. Once when I encountered him he was barechested—heavier, stockier than I had at first supposed. Possibly I should now revise his weight to one hundred and fifty. Done. The central male characters who are the heroes of his books are larger, heavier than he, for they must be sturdier, I suppose, to carry the burden of his consciousness. Tommy Wilhelm and Henderson are big men. Herzog weighs one hundred and seventy pounds. Sammler is tall.

As for other features of Bellow's body, much is made of his teeth and hair by scribblers on the run. They always speak of the gap between his two front teeth. Maybe they are *gap*-fetishists. And of course they always speak of his hair, which for many years has been silver. His eyes are brown.

Bellow began to compute the total wordage of my diary. Yes, since 1934, seventy-five or a hundred words a day, thirty thousand a year, about one million words by 1967—he did not carry forward the arithmetic on the spot; I did so afterward. Of what use was my diary? Well, for example, I said, if I were to write a fellow's biography I had a ready fund there from which to establish the connection of things by establishing their chronological order: writing a few words at the end of each day was a form of review, rereading what I had written was a second review. Clear enough in my mind forever that I had bought the book with Bellow's essay, "The Sealed Treasure," and left Vermont, and arrived at Tivoli, and whenever I reread those little entries I recalled again the glorious woman in the house at Tivoli, and Bellow standing at the window saying, "Why should somebody die because I'm nervous?"

Then, too, I could add details to my memory by rereading my letter file. For example, woodchucks fell into place that way. Bellow compared Frost to a woodchuck in his letter to me December 12, 1961—"Frost is a different kettle of woodchuck altogether"—and I knew Frost had that poem about a woodchuck; so I read it to see how it fit; and the notion eventually dawned upon me that Bellow was a woodchuck, too, especially when I began to become aware of woodchuck images in his writing. Old Taube has teeth "like a woodchuck . . . no arch but a straight line of teeth." A woodchuck is very smart. A woodchuck has the sense to hide, to conceal himself/ herself. "Thoreau saw a woodchuck at Walden, its eyes more fully awake than the eyes of any farmer."[7] The woodchucks have the sense to be hibernating when Humboldt comes "skedaddling dangerously" in his Buick. Bellow, like Frost's woodchuck (see epigraph), dives down under the farm. In Jerusalem, hearing of "an ancient cistern" under the floor of the Armenian church, he had yearned for its cool retreat; in the court of "the Greek portion of the Christian Quarter" he was "tempted to sit down and stay put for an aeon in the consummate mildness. The origin of this desire is obvious—it comes from the contrast between politics and peace. The slightest return of beauty makes you aware how deep your social wounds are, how painful it is to think continually of nothing but aggression and defense, superpowers, diplomacy, terrorism, war."[8] Crying for help to his father, Tommy Wilhelm grieves that he has

7. *Humboldt's Gift.*
8. "Reflections," *The New Yorker,* July 19, 1976, p. 37.

lived all his life too little like a woodchuck: "Let's suppose that all my life I had the wrong ideas about myself and wasn't what I thought I was. And wasn't even careful to take a few precautions, as most people do—like a woodchuck has a few exits to his tunnel." For Herzog "there were times when you wanted to creep into hiding, like an animal." Bellow knew what Frost was up to with those exits, tunnels, burrows. Escape! Spain, Rome, Yugoslavia, Italy, Dublin, the Dolomites, running off, fleeing, hiding, telephone down, mail mysteriously astray—What letter was that, Mark?

"What *chutzpah*," said Bellow, speaking of Frost's politics, "Frost's saying that if you want to know how he voted you have to read his Collected Works. When you get all through his Collected Works you'll find that he didn't vote for anybody."

We talked of revision. Stern applauded James for having revised everything for the New York edition. He became playful, dreaming up revisions. For example, The Sermon on the Mount Revisited for the New York edition, in which the author now amends as follows: "I don't know that I really feel that way about the meek any more." Stern urged Bellow to tell his little poem about the Polish girl. Bellow hesitated. Stern thought he was declining, as if he did not wish to recite on cue, but Bellow said no, he was only getting into the mood. He recited it. He recited it again on the following night. Pure sound, pure silliness. Unluckily he recited faster than I could write.

Bellow told a joke about the young man who was shy. For his wedding night a friend coached him, telling him to rub his bride's stomach while saying over and over, "I love you, I love you." The shy fellow followed his friend's instructions, rubbing his bride's stomach and saying over and over, "I love you, I love you." But after a period of time his bride stopped him, saying, "Lower," whereupon the young man resumed rubbing her stomach, saying over and over, "I love you, I love you," but in a lower voice.

The joke has a literary version. In a taxicab Ramona asks Herzog to feel how her heart is beating. Herzog takes her wrist, to count her pulse, "but she said, 'We are not young children, Professor,' and put his hand elsewhere."

ON THE FOLLOWING DAY I attended a conference at the Center for Continuing Education. The meeting was sponsored by the Institute of Politics of the John Fitzgerald Kennedy School of Government. It was one of the smallest conferences I ever attended—

eleven participants were announced, of whom seven appeared, and although we agreed upon many things and disagreed about others, made many plans, raised many questions, identified issues, and wonderfully spoke (my notes show) of "problems of medium-range immediacy," I never heard anything further.

That night a dinner was held for the conferees and spouses or invited friends on the twenty-fifth floor at 333 North Michigan Avenue. I was told that Bellow had been invited to that dinner at my "special request." The invitation to him was several weeks old—odd to hear, I thought, since he had told me on the phone from Morton's Steak House that he was surprised to hear from me; hadn't known I was coming to Chicago. During the evening I also heard that he had actually been invited at the "special request" of Mayor Arthur Naftalin of Minneapolis; or, again, at the "special request" of Adam Yarmolinsky, representing the Institute of Politics—certainly a peculiar necessity since Yarmolinsky (i.e., his Institute) as host for the dinner was under no obligation to make a special request of himself.

When I arrived on the twenty-fifth floor I had the brief illusion that things were clearer. Obviously the event was not Yarmolinsky's but Mayor Naftalin's, for it was Mayor Naftalin who now greeted everyone as he or she arrived, helping people off with their coats, leading them to cocktails, presiding at table, announcing his regret at someone's leaving early, helping him or her *on* with coats, and guiding them to the elevator, saying, "I'm so glad you could come, wish you could have stayed longer." Yet, *technically* our host was Charles Daly, Vice-President for Public Affairs of the University of Chicago. It was Daly who told me that Yarmolinsky (i.e., his Institute) was the sponsor or host of the dinner, who, in fact, several times *stressed* it. Naftalin gaily confessed later in the evening that he had all along been playing host without being put to the expense of it. "It's an old political trick," he said, "I've done it before."

Mayor Naftalin, who had been a professor at the University of Minnesota when I was a student there, mentioned several times our having been acquainted. I had no close memory of it. He was a jolly and quick-witted man, relaxed and shameless, whom Bellow found amusing. (Mayor Naftalin had been acquainted with Bellow at the University of Minnesota, he said.) He was one of those brilliant, active, effective managers of people and events all the more engaging for his modern liberality mixed with old downtown blarney. His heedlessness of language or indifference to the mere literal truth of things may be the envy of the literary man too much in love with the tools of his trade to abuse them. Perhaps Bellow sometimes longed to relax in Naftalin's way, for I heard him tell the physician's wife at table, "I never tell the literal truth about anything." Herzog himself reflects: "Strict and literal truthfulness was a trivial game and might even be a disagreeable neurotic affliction."

The Mayor flattered me by announcing in a loud voice his acquaintance with my writings, although it was in fact an acquaintance with only one book already fourteen years behind me. He somewhat angered me at another point, saying, "Oh, you have known Bellow a long time," embarrassing me before Bellow, who ought not to have the idea that his prospective biographer went about dropping his name. The Mayor made it sound as if I had boasted in the taxicab of my acquaintance with Bellow, but I had not ridden in the taxicab with the Mayor that night or any other (we had come from the Center to the twenty-fifth floor in *two* cabs); therefore I suspected for a moment that the Mayor was confusing me with Yarmolinsky, a theory soon punctured by his introducing Yarmolinsky to Bellow in the same general terms he had introduced Bellow and me—"Oh, you two have known each other for a long time." Yarmolinsky had told me that he had never met Bellow. Bellow had told me that he knew Yarmolinsky's *parents*. So much for politics.

After we had drunk some we sat to a dinner of roast beef, followed by a wide selection of desserts. Among old friends of Bellow who were present was a physician who had attended him in Minneapolis—a close reader of Joyce and a political radical with whom I felt instantly compatible. He was a good man for me to know if I became Bellow's biographer. A subject's medical history may tell worlds about him. Bellow spoke deferentially to the physician, saying, "I'm sure your literary ideas are more interesting to me than my physical history could have been to you."

The wife of the physician wore black. Sitting beside Bellow, she clung to him in an affectionate or admiring way, fully attentive to him, turning her back on her roast beef. At one point he said to her that Mrs. Kennedy, wife to the late President, had said to him, "I feel sorry for the author of *Herzog*," meaning, I take it, that the life of Herzog was the life of Bellow. Bellow said, "I would have argued with her, but the Secret Service was in the next room and I didn't want to raise my voice." I was pleased to hear him refer to Mrs. Kennedy as "Mrs. Kennedy."

When the conversation touched upon delicate points of politics I became somewhat wary. I thought it best, if I were to be Bellow's biographer, to establish myself with him along safer lines to start: I could better survive a political dispute later than sooner. Of Whittaker Chambers the physician said, "He was an insane psychotic." I, too, believed the worst of Chambers, but I was guarded on that subject in Bellow's presence—cautious, feeling out his opinions. Bellow was as tentative as I. Of Chambers he said only that "he did more harm as an editor of *Time* than he ever did as a Communist." Of Chambers's famous antagonist, Alger Hiss, Bellow said, "He's running around New York with chippies." Not much commitment there either way.

In the period ahead, as the question of Vietnam developed, I would have a difficult time knowing how to conduct myself in Bellow's presence: that is to say, I had a difficult time knowing where Bellow stood. I opposed the war absolutely. Presumably he, too, as a man against guns, opposed the war. Why then was he embattled with anti-war people when they met? That was a complicated question which took me awhile to answer. I would need to reread all Bellow to understand, for his mere life was merely tentative. Meanwhile the only related principle I adhered to was the principle of not telling Bellow where I stood.

At table he told of having seen the late Colonel McCormick, publisher of the Chicago *Tribune*, transfer himself from his automobile to his office building, emerging from a bullet-proof Cadillac, guarded by two "torpedoes" with pistols. Bellow was apparently close enough to Colonel McCormick to see that he had great bags under his weeping eyes—the physician supplied a medical name for this affliction.

Bellow's recounting this event remained with me. Each time I read it in my journal I wondered why it had so impressed him. Nine years later I came upon it again in *Humboldt's Gift*: Citrine's memory of the event is revived by the sight of a "garment" worn by the hoodlum Cantabile: "The last garment I had seen resembling this one was worn by the late Colonel McCormick. I was then about twelve years old. His limousine had stopped in front of the Tribune Tower, and two short men came out. Each man held two pistols, and they circled on the pavement, crouching low. Then, in this four-gun setting, the Colonel stepped out from his car in just such a tobacco-colored coat as Cantabile's and a pinch hat with gleaming harsh fuzz. The wind was stiff, the air pellucid, the hat glistened like a bed of nettles."

Assume the boy to be Bellow in the year 1927. Who was Colonel McCormick that a twelve-year-old boy should have observed him so keenly? Of course, the Colonel owned a printing press, a man of words, a writer, so to speak, a power in the city so fabulous that only four guns can keep him safe. If a boy had in himself the desire to write he might carry forever the memory of that chance encounter.

Someone pointed to the top of another skyscraper, the penthouse apartment of the publisher of the magazine *Playboy*, where, it was said, extremely amusing parties were held every night. Several persons expressed a determination to go. Bellow telephoned someone who could admit our group to the *Playboy* penthouse, but since the party did not begin until midnight our enthusiasm was dampened: the Mayor, the physician, and their wives were obliged to drive back to Minneapolis early in the morning. I said I hadn't much interest in untouchable girls running around in jockey shorts like Henderson in Africa. Bellow said I might be more interested if I were from Minneapolis; a provincial remark, I thought.

I mentioned to Bellow that I was at that moment considering writing an article for *Playboy* on golf, about which I knew nothing. I told him truthfully that I had been offered $2,000 for such an article. Bellow said I should certainly not accept that sum when for the same effort I could receive $10,000 from "other magazines." What other magazines? I did not inquire. Did Bellow think I received such fees? Or was he revealing that *he* commanded such fees—counterboasting my $60,000 of the night before? For golf? About which I knew nothing? Nothing I knew was worth $10,000 to a magazine. Would *Playboy* care for an interesting article about American literature 1885–1892? Since Bellow viewed $10,000 as so small a sum I once again began to feel economically inferior to him, unworthy to be his biographer, a man of a different and lower class. I cast about in my mind for new funds for my father to invest.

Mayor Naftalin told of having seen Bellow's play, *The Last Analysis*, in New York, of having risen in the theater and called out "Author! Author!" but his wife contradicted him, saying he had done no such thing. All that they could agree on was that they had seen the play in New York—"in the antique filth of the Belasco," as Charlie Citrine was yet to call it, whose own play, *Von Trenck*, in the same theater, earned fabulous sums for everybody, as *The Last Analysis* did not. This was the play *Life* accused of having accumulated no prizes, while a scribbler in the San Francisco newspaper described it as "a play that bombed so badly on Broadway that no one can remember the title."[9]

Perhaps the Mayor's enthusiasm for the play had increased with time. In retrospect he cheered. It grew upon him during two years of thought. The ideals of Bummidge, hero of the play, were the Mayor's own ideals when he entered politics. But then, like Bummidge, he sank into the reality of his profession. "I'm the instrument of a purpose beyond ordinary purpose," Bummidge declares, seeking to recover his point of origin. "I may be the only man on the Eastern Seaboard with a definitely higher purpose. What a thing to get stuck with!" Oh, to be normal! To be happy with money only! To be relieved of the quest for self-knowledge!

But Bummidge cannot abandon himself. In *The Last Analysis* he administers mental medicine to himself. Of course, since he had been a performing artist, star of stage and television, it is natural enough for him now to make a *show* of his buried mind. Performance is his medium. Bummidge will beam his psychoanalysis by closed-circuit television across Manhattan to a conference of the American Psychiatric Association at the Waldorf. This comic interlude has been approved by the Program Committee, remembering Bummidge. "There was a time when my cousin Bummidge was king of the networks—the greatest comedian of his time. Now look at him, almost destroyed by his ideas, mental experiments—home-brewed psychoanalysis. Poor has-been."

Friends and relations play out roles with Bummidge. Sometimes they impersonate themselves; sometimes they act out someone else's life with Bummidge—his cousin, his sister, his aunt, his secretary, his mistress, an old friend, a "scientific collaborator, formerly a ratcatcher," and what they're catching now is Bummidge's soul and essence. Bummidge will now find out what he's been doing all his life in the role of entertainer. Psychoanalysis will also be literary

9. Maitland Zane in the San Francisco *Chronicle*, May 14, 1968.

explication. And Bummidge, after all is said, will tell us who he is, even as Bellow might: "I bless the day when I discovered how abnormal I was. I read all the books, and never forgetting that I was an actor, a comedian, I formed my own method. I learned to obtain self-knowledge by doing what I best knew how to do, acting out the main events of my life, dragging repressed material into the open by the sheer force of drama. I'm not solely a man but a man who is also an artist, and an artist whose sphere is comedy."

Out of distress, out of the desire to dispel distress with laughter, comes the comedy of Bummidge. In the process of making his comedy he makes other people laugh, too, and he takes the money paid to him as his reward. However, since it was never the money he mainly sought, he is always in trouble with it. He has made no plans for it. He is inept in caring for it. His entourage has sucked him broke. Everybody is into him. "And now, with a secretary who used to be a bunny in a Playboy Club, and a collaborator who used to be a ratcatcher . . . now you spend your last dough on a closed-circuit TV broadcast to a bunch of specialists at the American Psychiatric Association."

After a certain period of self-study Bummidge reports: "The disease I discovered in myself, I call Humanitis. An emotional disorder of our relation to the human condition. Suddenly, being human is too much for me. I faint, and stagger. *He enacts the sick man. Holds dialogue with himself:* 'What's the matter, Bummidge? Don't you like other human beings?' 'Like them! I adore them! Only I can't bear them.' 'I love 'em like a dog. So ardent, so smoochy. Wagging my tail. This sick, corrupt emotion leaks out of me.' I don't have the strength to bear my feelings. *Lecturing:* This is the weakness of my comedy. When the laughing stops, there's still a big surplus of pain."

The play is ending. Bummidge's psychoanalysis is completed. He looks upon his work—he was his own psychoanalyst, his own cleric, he might as well be his own literary critic, too: "I am so moved! What a struggle I've had. It took me so long to get through the brutal stage of life. And when I was through it, the mediocre stage was waiting for me. And now that's done with, and I am ready for the sublime. *He raises his arm in a great gesture.* CURTAIN." Bellow, like Bummidge, retaining after each work his own surplus of pain, goes each time to new labor. Pain produces comedy. "Yes," said Bellow, in an interview given at about the time of *The Last Analysis*, "because I got very tired of the solemnity of complaint, altogether impatient with complaint. Obliged to choose between complaint and comedy, I choose comedy, as more energetic, wiser, and manlier. This is really one reason why I dislike my own early novels. I find them plaintive, sometimes querulous. *Herzog* makes comic use of complaint."[10]

I LEFT the dinner party with Bellow and Vice-President Daly. Daly's car was below. In view of Daly's being ever-so-slightly heavy-lidded from drinking I asked him whether he was a "careful driver" or whether perhaps he preferred that Bellow drive. He said he could drive. To keep alive the subject of the danger of driving, especially after drinking, I remarked that I supposed we were not far from the point where Herzog and June had suffered their accident after leaving the aquarium. Daly replied to my question very specifically, which rather surprised Bellow, who apparently had not been aware that Daly had read *Herzog* so closely.

Daly drove me to the Center for Continuing Education. I was perfectly prepared to be dragged "through the streets at all hours of the night" like Stern (according to Susan), but Bellow made no offer to drag me, offering only civilities at parting, asking me to extend his regards to his friend, my colleague, Wright Morris, and I said I would. Perhaps I slightly hesitated, for in the act of rolling up his window he paused and said, "You don't have to if you don't want to."

No, I said, it wasn't that, I was only remembering his letter of a year ago or more telling of having "blown up a valuable friendship" with Morris. "No problem," I said to Bellow, once more expressing my hope, as I had expressed it over the years, that he would come to teach at San Francisco State.

THE HOUR was early—not more than 10:30—and I was once again alone in one hundred and seventeen rooms at the Center for Continuing Education. I wrote up my journal. I made a diagram of our seating arrangement at dinner, to bring back memories afterward. Even so, I was left with an irresistible urge to talk to someone about my evening. I telephoned Susan Bellow. In her opinion the hour was late. Wasn't it? Not too late to talk on the phone, they don't take the wires down at night. She reproved my sarcasm. I didn't blame her.

10. "Saul Bellow: An Interview," *The Paris Review*, Winter 1966, p. 62.

We agreed not to talk about Bellow. She said she was unhappy about his having called off his appointment with Daniel that day.

He had to write, I said.

So that he could go out to dinner tonight, she said, with you and Daly—two grown men who wouldn't have been the least bit disappointed if he hadn't appeared.

His vice-president asked him, I said, perhaps Bellow felt the need, after all, to oblige the vice-president of the place where goodies came from.

Susan asked whether anyone was with us.

Six men and three women and Daly and Bellow and me, I said.

Was a woman with Saul?—that was what she meant.

"No," I said. I hoped she wouldn't ask me about the night before. She said, "How about last night?"

"No," I said.

Susan seemed to want me to know that she was "not unhappy." However, she did not say that she was happy. She said she felt "constrained" talking to me; she feared I would retain things; she had been reading *Twentyone Twice* since her visit to her psychiatrist, and some of the things her psychiatrist had suggested were coming up true.

"You talked with your psychiatrist about *me*?" I incredulously asked.

"About writers," she said.

"All writers are lovely people," I said. (Of a certain writer someone said, "Oh, I met him once. He seemed nice enough." "We all do," Bellow replied, "until you get to know us.")[11]

Susan spoke freely in starts; then became cautious again. Constrained. We talked about writers in general. She amused me by telling me that when she and Bellow were in need of a housemaid in New York they hired a lady from an agency run by Norman Mailer's mother. "It was called an agency," said Susan, "but it was a slave mart." She observed that Ellison and his wife were "cool" to them— to the Bellows—in New York. "He wrote us a very strange note when Daniel was born. It was clear they didn't want to see us."

"Cool to you," I said. "He was rude *and* cool to me in Boston."

"They were *both* rude and cool to us in New York," she said.

"*He* was rude to me in Boston," I said, "and they were *both* rude

11. "Mr. Bellow Considers His Planet," *Life*, April 3, 1970, p. 60.

to me in Los Angeles." I told her that I intended soon to move to Purdue University. I would be near Bellow, the Sterns, and her.

"Your getting to know me is only your way of getting close to Saul," she said.

"Not at all," I said. "I have an altogether different kind of interest in you from my interest in him."

Philosophically she said, "The best affairs are unplanned."

She said that when Bellow became angry at her he was capable of blaming her behavior on her being "a Lake Shore Jew." I was confused and disappointed to hear this, nor would it ever cease to plague me. "I'm not up on Chicago geography," I said, "the lake is east . . ."

Well, explained Susan, hers was a comfortable background, quite unlike his. Her father was a physician, she was from the right side of the tracks, so to speak, and Bellow from the other side of the tracks; assuming a Jewish railroad.

I said I thought that that was a bad way for Bellow to speak. These writers were a comedy, I said—the mother of the radical ran a slave mart, the black writer loved guns, and the beautiful Jewish writer was anti-Semitic. Bellow! He who would in the following year win the B'nai B'rith Heritage Award! And eight years later the B'nai B'rith America's Legacy Award—a silver medallion! Only in America. "I'm going to have to track down things like that if I become his biographer," I said. I said that I was prepared to spend ten years writing Bellow's biography.

"He might be dead by then," she said.

"I don't like to think about that," I said.

We talked until my elbows quivered with fatigue. Susan used the word "constrained" several times—constrained by my biographical intentions, although I tried to reassure her, telling her that when I should finally begin in earnest to gather information for the biography of Bellow (assuming that I had his permission in the first place) I should gather material openly only; I should do nothing in a sleuthing or underhand manner.

"Aren't you gathering it now?" she said.

"I don't know what I'm doing now," I said. "He didn't give me permission to do anything. I believe I'm off the job. He didn't even receive my letter from France."

"Did you write him from France?" she asked. "Why shouldn't he have received it?"

"He said he didn't," I said.

"Then you don't know," she said.

"We have so much in common," I said, "why don't I just drop over?"

No, she said, she was somewhat vulnerable these days on moral and legal grounds in connection with the divorce.

"I'm not planning anything immoral or illegal," I said.

"I could lose Daniel," she said.

"Do you suppose Saul would want custody of Daniel?" I asked. "Do you know what Boswell asked Johnson? 'If, Sir, you were shut up in a castle, and a newborn child with you, what would you do?'"

"What did he do?"

"He said, 'Why, Sir, I should not much like my company,' but he'd rear the child, feed it, give it fresh air—and then there's a whole lot of discussion about the value of hot water."

"The doorman would be suspicious," Susan said. "He might mention it to the wrong person." Indeed, something of the sort had already happened in *Herzog*. "What is this? Herzog had thought," reading a letter from a former student, now confidante to Madeleine, "Is she going to tell me that Madeleine is going to have a child? Gersbach's child! No! How wonderful—what luck for me. If she has a kid out of wedlock, I can petition for Junie's custody."

"Why not come over here?" I inquired. "I have one hundred and seventeen rooms and no doorman. Are we going to let a doorman get in the way of literary biography?" No such luck. "No," thinks Herzog, "Madeleine was not pregnant. She'd be far too clever to let that happen. She owed her survival to intelligence." Our silences grew longer and longer. Our hot line cooled. We hung up.

SUNDAY MORNING I telephoned the Sterns from the airport to say good-bye. In the telephone booth I found three dyed eggs and I realized the day was Easter. Gay answered the phone, greeting me in the warmest, friendliest way, and I thought *Boy I sure turned her on!* But she had thought it was Bellow, making the first of his four or five daily calls. Her enthusiastic manner made me think she was perhaps not so down on Bellow as Susan thought, perhaps didn't *mind* his dragging her husband through the streets at all hours.

Stern had a sore throat. He could barely speak. Nevertheless, he spoke to me, urging me to remember to record the *source* of every comment about Bellow. "Don't let things just enter your mind indiscriminately," he said. "Don't say 'somebody said this . . . somebody said that,' either attribute it to an actual person or say it on your own." He talked to me as if everything had been decided, as if I already *was* Bellow's biographer—game time, here we go, a few final words from the coach—quite as if Bellow had looked me square in the eye and said Yes.

"He'd never say Yes," Stern croaked.

"The other day you said he'd never say No," I said.

"Right," said Stern, who knew him far better than I. Thus my spirits lifted with the airplane, flying back to San Francisco. I was jubilant, exhilarated, slightly high, as if I were inhaling oxygen from the emergency mask overhead. I could see it now. The whole thing seemed possible because Stern thought it was. Stern the bolsterer, Stern the encourager. He was befogging the situation with optimism.

On the airplane I read in *The Paris Review* an interview with the playwright Edward Albee. I had never met Albee. I had no known prejudice for him or against him. I noticed how freely I read, taking him at his word, never having met or known any member of his family, neither young son nor old, nor castaway wife nor *bonne amie* nor friend nor the wife of his friend nor physician nor associated mayors or vice-presidents nor bitter old Minneapolis acquaintances in barber shops nor shy effeminate musicians in restaurants. Those were the ideal circumstances for writing biography—knowing nobody, never having laid eyes on the central figure.

Yet it was surely true, as John Silber reminded me in a letter, that Socrates and Samuel Johnson were written up creatively by friends of their living presence. Perhaps no rules have been established. Maybe it is itself a creative thing.

IN SAN FRANCISCO, following up Bellow's request, I spoke two days later with Wright Morris. "Bellow asked me to extend his greetings," I said.

"And that's what you're doing," Morris formally said, a little chill to his voice. He could keep a long silence. He did so now. He was later a teacher to my daughter, Hester, who admired him, respected him, thought him wonderfully contained—a monologist of a high order, she tells me, a marvel of dramatic silence. "Well," he said at last, "he could have done that for himself. There are good phone connections between here and there, I think, and he's not a man these days who really has to revert to the pony express." He became regretful, thawing a trifle, and he permitted himself to smile at me sympathetically. "Yes, you're only the poor rider."

"You're the only person in the whole city of San Francisco he especially asked for," I said.

"I'm pleased with that," Morris said.

"I feel that I'm doing the right thing."

"I wish he wasn't so distracted he could sustain this a little more on his own. He could write a letter now and then, that sort of thing, those things are not impossible to do."

I tried to explain to him that Bellow was overwhelmed with communication, torrents of mail, sometimes six telegrams from the same party, and beyond that he was probably not so completely luxurious in his finances that he could just pick up the long-distance telephone at will. The latter point interested Morris. He probed. He had had an image of Bellow's living in wealth and serenity. "Did you see him out at his home?" Morris asked. "Or did you just meet him somewhere and have a drink? He's probably—*probably* still in that apartment on the lake front."

"It was dark," I said.

"It wasn't too dark to see the lake, was it? You might not have noticed it over there at the end of Fifty-Fifth Street . . ."

"We're by the ocean here," I said, "but I have no sense of noticing the ocean."

"I only ask because it's a pretty plush place there."

"It wasn't a plush place I was in," I said. "It was a small, cramped apartment."

"You don't say so. Small and cramped but beautifully furnished, I suppose."

"I don't remember. He sat on a chair."

"Oh, he kept a chair in his apartment, did he?" Wright Morris inquired. "It's beginning to sound to me as if something has changed. Did you meet his wife?"

"Lunch," I said.

"Lunch?" he replied, waiting for me to continue.

"I hate to be gossiping," I said.

"We're not gossiping. This is a man we both know. This is of some concern to me."

"Frankly," I said, "I don't believe he's living with his wife right now."

"It's odd that we should just stumble into it this way, meet on a street corner"—though we were in his office—"and look down and notice that one of us has a wooden leg. That would make quite a difference because they were living together when I saw them just about the first of November, in that apartment on the lake front."

"From something I heard," I said, "he's only been in this present apartment since December."

"This present, small, cramped apartment with one single chair," he said.

"It's only temporary," I said.

"Well then," said Wright Morris, "that's what happened."

Chapter Four

RENEWED BY Stern's encouraging Easter message, believing myself to be the strongest possible candidate for biographer regardless
of any depression or negativism I may have felt at other hours in
Chicago, I began to organize the journal I had begun to write that
evening in the Center. I began with the venereal taxicab driver.

I wrote gratefully to Stern for his boost to me at the moment I
needed it—"Right now I am trying to think my way into the far
future, how to compose the Life of Bellow, how to relate it to my
own schedule of life; with occasional phrases running trials as I
compose my dedication to Richard G. Stern; for without you it
would indeed be impossible; you have first entitlement." Pumping
myself full of encouragement, I could see my idea as reality on the
basis of Stern's having seen it so. He replied: "Avanti with Vita
Bellorum, oops. A gray, Canadian morn, the old Jew humped for
the dying coals, an infant's cry shivers the frail timbers. 'We'll call
him Saul . . .' Years later, in a '63 Chrysler, ye old scribe conversed
with a muchal friend. "Dick-o boy-o, you know what became of
that babe . . .' OK, that's your lead, take it. The least I can do for a
dedication."

I received also a sweet short note from Mayor Naftalin on station-
ery of the City of Minneapolis, who said that he planned "to go to
the Library" and read all my work "when the campaign is over."

I do not know what he was running for, or whether he won or lost.
He was not the first political person to tell me he planned to read

my work as soon as his politics was done. The first was George Christopher, mayor of San Francisco, who, having sworn me in as a commissioner of art (a title to make Bellow wince), said he intended to read everything I had ever written as soon as he ceased to be mayor.

The third such political person to say such a thing to me was Governor Edmund G. Brown, Sr. (Democrat, California), whom I met when he was running for reelection to his office in 1962, who said to me that when he was finished with politics, or politics finished with him, he intended truly to get down to the serious business of reading all the high-class literature of the world, beginning with mine. I believe that he believed that he would, because he did not like to think of himself as telling a lie.

The fourth and final political person ever to tell me that he intended to read me was Richard Nixon (first president I ever met; first president ever to *resign*), who said to me in 1962, when he was campaigning against Governor Brown, that as soon as he was done with political life he intended to read my books. At first it appeared that he was done with political life that very year. But instead of lying back and reading my books he stayed right there in the political midst, working toward the presidency, an office he achieved, so that he wasn't done with political life until 1973, when he stepped from office, and, true to his promise, no doubt, retired to the Western seaside with his arms full of my books and has been reading them ever since.

OF COURSE I wrote to the central figure himself, sending him a copy of the letter I had sent him from France July 31 of the previous year, and telling him that I had passed his greetings to Wright Morris. I told him that I had spent "weeks . . . writing up my visit with you March 25 and thereabouts," so that if he wished me not to do it he must for God's sake cry Stop. He cried no such thing, but wrote me a postcard a month later, "Dear Mark, See you in September. I'm off with mss for the Summer. Which will be a pleasant one for us all I trust. Saul."

"Off" where? He didn't say. Spain, Rome, Yugoslavia? The Dolomites. Block Island off the Rhode Island shore? Stern once told me that Bellow sometimes took a ferry to Block Island; the same island to which Benjamin Franklin sometimes *rowed*. "He had a girl on the island," Stern said, but whether he meant Bellow or Franklin I never knew. Anyhow, fleeing, "vanishing over the horizon," as he once put it to a friend of mine: "In the spring I expect to be somewhere in Spain, calmly lying down under an olive tree." Charlie Citrine's brother urges him to take up residence "in one of the cheap countries like Yugoslavia or Turkey," work on his "scribbles" there, "and tell the Chicago gang to fuck itself."

And with what "mss"? Did he mean two? Perhaps, for his story, "The Old System," was published in *Playboy* the following January, and "Mosby's Memoirs" in *The New Yorker* July 20, 1968. I wrote to him praising both. Regarding "Mosby's Memoirs" he replied to me, "I see, looking back at the vanished years, that I wrote few stories and that I seem to have used them as 'scale models' for bigger jobs. For that reason I was a bit worried about Mosby; I wondered what big job it would lead to."

The question of "The Old System" is less difficult. Dr. Braun seems to me to be clearly a 'scale model' for Mr. Sammler, Bellow's hero of advancing age, the man who has seen the worst: Mr. Sammler has come to America from his own grave; his wife had been shot to death beside him; the man of control, all knowing, all compassionate, illusionless, he who speaks with "earth-departure objectivity," returned from the dead to treasure this earth, this life, inexpressibly sad, objectively hopeful for the world, this globe.

Mr. Sammler has known "the totalitarian experience," a term Bellow uses in his book of Israel. Of certain Jews someone says "their totalitarian experience matured their souls as well as toughened their minds. Bitter experience has given them a wisdom too scarce to be wasted."[1] That experience was Sammler's, and Bellow its medium to a society whose holocausts were already slipping its mind. The twentieth century, Citrine observes, "has seen everything. After the holocausts, you can't blame it for lacking interest in private difficulties." But if the world has grown numb to its own madness then Bellow is compelled to serve as the world's memory. In *To Jerusalem and Back* he tells of the jury foreman in Chicago who cannot believe that guiltless persons under Nazism were imprisoned without being charged. "What is 'known' in civilized coun-

1. "Reflections," *The New Yorker*, July 12, 1976, p. 80.

tries, what people may be assumed to 'know,' is a great mystery. . . .
A great deal of intelligence can be invested in ignorance when the
need for illusion is deep."[2]

Herzog was past, Bummidge had broken through, every Bellow
hero was scale model enough, and Mr. Sammler soon the sum of
them all. So I felt. Bellow was past fifty and growing.

I WAS ENCOURAGED by his saying that he expected to see me in
September. His quick postcard had the faintest sound of an invitation, and I thought of myself all summer as Bellow's biographer.

September arrived. I was now at Purdue University, a century-old
institution at West Lafayette, Indiana, two or three hours by automobile from Chicago. I was hopeful, by this proximity, of seeing Bellow much more often than I had when I was living in San Francisco.
I thought I would now visit him frequently. But September departed,
and I had not budged.

I was finally able to overcome my inertia—my fears, I suppose,
my hesitations, my sense of Bellow's reluctance—when a colleague
at Purdue asked me to help him move his household from one part
of town to another. We could easily do it on a Saturday, and not too
many hours into Sunday, laughing and sweating and drinking beer,
nothing was really heavy except the piano and ten thousand books.
My colleague had never owned a house—he was at the mercy of
landlords. Piano, books, many children! I could not say No. Yet I
could not say Yes. And when I pleaded *literary business* in Chicago
he ordered me to go.

I could not reach Bellow by telephone at the august or prestigious
Committee on Social Thought, nor by leaving a message with his
former wife, Susan, nor at that small, cramped apartment which
Wright Morris and I in our collaborative ignorance had never actually located—from which, in any case, as I soon learned, he had
moved to a high, fine apartment on the twelfth floor of a building
overlooking a park. I do not know what park. I remember saying to
Bellow when I finally reached it, "You can see the soccer games
free." He took me to another window, saying, "From this window I
can see the *lake* free."

I reached Stern by telephone, who invited me to come, who

2. Ibid., July 19, 1976, p. 54.

assured me that Bellow would be in town and available. When I pressed him regarding my standing as biographer he said I would probably not receive any "explicit cooperation" from Bellow. He said, "Saul mentioned this the other day . . . every writer's life is his own, that's how he put it."

Very well, I said, I understand: he doesn't want to see me.

No, no, said Stern, "I wouldn't be responsible for such a broad statement. He *does* want to see you, or anyhow he doesn't *not* want to see you, he's both flattered and reluctant, let's put it that way."

My daughter Hester and I left West Lafayette early on a Friday afternoon. The iron-gray sky was a hundred times harder on my eyes than California sunshine, my sunglasses were useless, and I would be plagued all weekend by eyestrain. My taking my sunglasses on and off so often amused Hester, who speculated that I was neurotic. I was happy to have her companionship. She was a senior in high school, and this weekend she would be my chaperone, reducing my possibilities for mischief, preventing my wandering from the task I had assigned myself; from which, in any case, I was inclined to stray unless Bellow soon became more distinctly cordial.

Without too much difficulty we arrived at the Sterns. The lake was always east. My eyes were scorched from the drive. Gay was just returning from shopping. Soon Stern came down from one of the floors above to help her carry the bags in. He wore moccasins and a somewhat ill-fitting overcoat sent to him by his father, who had inherited it as the result of a mistake in a restaurant cloakroom. Stern was afflicted by the same "semiannual bronchitis" he had been suffering from on Easter morning, and he occasionally coughed up quantities of phlegm, running to find a place to spit. In adult company everyone pretended not to notice, but his youngest child, Nick, age six, clearly expressed his displeasure at the sound, holding his hands over his ears.

Bellow was to come for dinner. Meanwhile, Stern took Hester and me for a tour of the campus of the university. At one point he called to someone just entering another car, "Richard, where's my book?" —Susanne Langer's *Mind: An Essay on Human Feeling*, as it turned out. The man called Richard began to discuss the book with Stern, neglecting to close the door of the car he had begun to enter. The driver began to drive the car away, door open. Richard on foot trotted after it, while Stern drove slowly beside him, driving, discussing the book, pursuing the car with the flapping door.

When we arrived again at the Sterns' house Bellow had not yet appeared, nor had he telephoned. I was lodged in a bedroom on the top floor. Facing my bed was a Miro print of a leaping fish, a red sun, a field of green. I enjoyed the Miro sun but not the real one—my window was shadeless and my eyes still burned from the highway.

As often happens, however, a strange room soon becomes familiar, and by the end of my stay I was thoroughly at home, which is to say, deeply involved in the events of the house, taking telephone messages (hoping for Bellow) mainly from children for children, and receiving callers at the door, usually children seeking Stern children, of whom there were four. Hester became especially friendly with Chris and Kate, who were near to her own age, and the first night remained awake talking with them until four o'clock in the morning. The second night I was myself awake and abroad until four in the morning on an uncertain, dismal, vague, failed quest.

Bellow did not appear for dinner. The guest who did appear was Edward Shils; sociologist, author, and editor, if I heard correctly, of a magazine called *Nirvana*. Bellow has mentioned Shils as a "friend," and I am therefore especially interested in Shils's politics. I have heard him called conservative or reactionary. But Stern has written of Shils as an advocate of "the politics of civility, the politics of adjustment—small gains, large compromise and larger tolerance."[3]

Shils was a red-haired man, and he lisped, so that when I heard him deplore lisping in someone else I was puzzled whether he meant it as a kind of satire of himself, or whether, in fact, which was certainly possible, he was unable to hear his own. In several cases he was critical of people on the grounds of their physical characteristics, and he seemed to take a dim view of almost everyone whose name was mentioned. I did not know who they were—they were mainly Chicago people. He spoke with an odd accent, as if he were learning British.

When I complained to Stern that I had not instantly warmed to

3. In *The Books in Fred Hampton's Apartment* (London: Hamish Hamilton, 1974), p. 25.

Shils (perhaps I was fretting about Bellow's failure to appear) he replied that Shils was extremely tired, that he had recently been commuting between the University of Chicago and one of the universities of London. His twelve-year-old son was living in England, and his wife lived on yet a third continent.

For dinner we had "Chinese turkey" and a fantastic dessert of chocolate and rum. No word came from Bellow. I felt certain that he was avoiding me. No, said Stern, this had happened in the past "two or three times." Stern constantly reassured me—Bellow had other problems, big problems, of that I could be sure. But if this kind of incident had occurred, I asked, only "two or three times" in the past why was I one of the two or three victims. For example, what had I done so violently to offend the law of averages that of the dozens and dozens of letters I had written from France in the summer of 1966 (every one of which had been received in America by its intended recipient) only my letter to Bellow had failed of its destination?

About ten o'clock a man arrived named Lewontin. His face was somewhat familiar. I couldn't place it, and I mulled it over. Hester, passing through the room, instantly recognized him as the man we had seen that afternoon trotting after his automobile. He had brought with him the book by Langer, which he and Stern had read deeply and which they now discussed with absorption. I was unable to follow them. Lewontin was a "population geneticist" who had solved one of the two major problems facing population geneticists, but what those problems were I do not know. By midnight, when Bellow had neither appeared nor telephoned nor sent a message in any other shape, I went upstairs to my bed.

SATURDAY MORNING I arose somewhat tired, for the light through the shadeless window had kept me awake. Gay Stern served me a fine breakfast. Dick was in his robe, reading the *Sun-Times*. The day was gray and slightly damp. No word had come from Bellow. Things with Bellow seemed so emotionally and logistically complicated that I had decided in the night to give up—it was truly as Stern had said, a man could never be himself in the presence of his biographer: my biographical ambition had ruined a friendship.

Yes, said Stern, true that a man was inhibited in the presence of his biographer—he *had* said that—but that wasn't the problem of the moment. The problem now was family distraction. Susan. Daniel.

I was called by a child to the telephone. It was Bellow. Delighted to hear from him, I appreciated his calling, I'd been in Chicago since yesterday afternoon—no, no, hadn't missed him at all, Shils and Lewontin last night, lovely guys. I talked as if I had endless errands here in the big city, although it was *one of* my "main purposes," I confessed, to see him if neither he nor I was too busy; I could perhaps spare him a quiet corner of my day; saving face a little. Not for nothing had I lived in Japan.

"I woke in the middle of the night," said Bellow. "I had indigestion. Why did I have indigestion?"

"Not from eating dinner with me," I said.

"Because I forgot Dick's dinner party. I don't keep any written memoranda, but I seldom forget engagements." He said he would be at the Sterns' house at four o'clock in the afternoon.

Hester and I drove to the Art Institute. Then to Marshall Field's for lunch, she to shop, I to stand in the television department watching the World Series in color. Later I asked Stern whether Bellow were interested in games. "Yes," said Dick, "philosophy and fucking."

Games indeed! The earnestness of many people to find a systematic philosophy in Bellow's work adds to the laughter. Bellow might say of his fiction, as Frost said of his own poetry, that "I got my truth of feeling in." Not *all* the truth—a "big surplus of pain" remains for the next work.

Bellow's seeming philosophy attracts innocence in the way prizes and awards attract critical superlatives. My own first experience of the innocent earnestness of readers occurred when I conducted a class discussion of his story "A Sermon by Doctor Pep." To my amazement, students received "Doctor" Pep's stream-of-consciousness not only as if it were a rational system, but as if it were Bellow's own. They took the portrait for the painter. But to write about a nutty orator in Bughouse Square, Chicago, is not to *be* one.

As far as I know, the only critic to insist upon the distinction between Bellow as novelist and Bellow as philosopher is Nathan Scott, who does it so well that I cannot resist quoting him at length: "Mr. Bellow is perhaps himself the outstanding 'theoretician' amongst the major novelists of our period, and his books are drenched in speculation. This is not to say that he conceives the novel to be an essentially expository medium or that he is a 'philosophical novelist,' in the usual sense of that term, for the immediate stuff of his art is not an affair of (as Lionel Trilling would say) those 'pellets of intellection' which are the material of systematic thought: it is, rather, an affair of enormously larky and vital characters and of the interesting relationships into which they are brought with one another and with the world of the American metropolis. But these characters themselves are personages whose most fundamental interest is a 'theoretical' interest, and therein, Mr. Bellow seems to feel, is the real wellspring of their humanity."[4]

BELLOW ARRIVED at the Sterns' at 4:30 with Daniel, now three and a half years old, whom I had not seen in nearly two years, though we had talked on the phone in March. Daniel's face was ivory-white, fragile, and his hair was brown and curly, whereupon the question arose whether Bellow's hair had been curly when he was a child, just as the question had arisen in Morton's Steak House with Gregory. I don't know why. Daniel had recently had the dreadful experience of swallowing a lethal quantity of "baby aspirin," of being taken to the hospital and forced to vomit. The accident had seemed to be more than an accident—he had had to climb to a certain height, open the medicine cabinet with a key, swallow the aspirin, and then go tell someone what he had done.

Bellow wore a porkpie hat, his gray or silver hair flowing free where it could, and a gray tie which Stern examined, saying, "It would go well with a pink suit." Bellow replied, "If I could find a pink suit I'd buy it." He complained of Susan's spending. "Whenever I call for Daniel she hands me a bunch of bills. Some of the things I'm not responsible for. Others she pays more for than she should." Madeleine's charge accounts drove Herzog out of his mind. Trying to paint the house at Ludeyville, "time and again he was brought down from the ladder to the telephone. Madeleine's checks were bouncing. . . . The dress shop just phoned—Milly Crozier. Five hundred bucks on a maternity outfit. Who's going to be born—Louis Quatorze?"

4. *Three American Moralists* (Notre Dame, Ind.: University of Notre Dame Press, 1973), p. 107.

We sat on the steps of the porch. Down the street some girls were burning leaves. Stern said the burning was illegal—he objected to it—but Bellow welcomed it, saying it was something for Daniel to see, and we walked down the street. Bellow was inattentive to me, uncomfortable, not himself. I tried to think it was his domestic problem, not the presence of his biographer. Yet sometimes, when he spoke, he glanced at me sharply to see if I were taking him in, if I understood him, or were capable of doing so, as if he were contemplating telling me something (which he was: tomorrow) while wondering if I could receive it, or whether it would rise into nothing like the smoke of the burning leaves.

These were black girls. Three white men advancing on black girls. It looked fishy. A man came out of a house, as if suspiciously, or so I thought, but he was known to Stern, who introduced him to me as Abt. Stern told me later that Abt was head of the Chicago Anti-Defamation League. The name "Abt" appears in *Dangling Man*. I said so. Bellow gazed at me. "I haven't read that book in a long time," he said. Yes, it was more than twenty years old. Bellow and Abt compared their lives in Chicago. Bellow had lived in Chicago "off and on" since 1924, he said. I thought of all the traveling I'd need to do if I were to follow the path of Bellow's life in the conventional biographical way—Canada to Chicago, Minneapolis, New York, Tivoli, Paris, a house in southern California with the whole cast of *Herzog*, and many points between: later he told Jane Howard of *Life* that he had lived "upwards" of two hundred places. "I guess I could list them all for you, if I felt like it, but I don't," he told her. How could I check out two hundred places? Maybe I could get a grant. I could ask him many things to help me reduce my traveling, but he had told the lady on the twenty-fifth floor that he never told the literal truth about anything. "What years did you live in Montreal?" I couldn't ask him a question like that. It wasn't the kind of conversation he enjoyed. He wouldn't care to list things for me. He cared to talk, make jokes, speculate, gossip, try out theories and opinions, prejudices and devotions. For specific facts you must go to a certified public accountant.

For tonight, Bellow had been invited to a cocktail party and felt at liberty to invite me in turn, guaranteeing me that Harold Rosenberg would be there, and a Frenchman who was a renowned expert on Marxism. However, I had promised the Sterns to take them to din-

ner. Stern said that I was foolish to neglect my main business in
Chicago. Besides, he had bronchitis. I insisted, however, and Bellow
appeared unhappy. It may be that he would have preferred my company to Daniel's. "These children's outings," Herzog found, "were
always exhausting. Often, after a day with Marco, Moses had to put
a cold compress on his eyes, and lie down." Off went Bellow with
Daniel, and I with the Sterns to dine on whitefish at the Courthouse
Restaurant in Harper Square. Here I had come with Susan. "I was
here once," I blurted.

"With whom?" Gay asked.

"Oh, with a friend," I said. "I forget who."

But possibly Susan had told Gay of our luncheon, for Gay had
been, she said, "Susan's ear" during the critical early period of the
Bellows' separation. I asked whether a reconciliation were possible.
"Susan thinks so," said Gay, as if she herself doubted it.

Whether the Sterns knew of my momentary warmth of friendship
with Susan I have never known. No telling who might tell what to
whom. Or whether, if anyone did, and Bellow knew, it would have
damaged me in his eyes. Poor Herzog, he had learned about Madeleine's affair with Valentine Gersbach from Lucas Asphalter, the
zoologist, who heard it from a young woman—"a lab assistant here
who sits with your little girl, and she's been telling me about your
wife."

"What about her?"

"And Valentine Gersbach. He's always there, on Harper
Avenue."

"Sure. I know. He's the only reliable person on the scene. I
trust him. He's been an awfully good friend."

"Yes, I know—I know, I know," said Asphalter. His pale
round face was freckled, and his eyes large, fluid, dark, and, for
Moses's sake, bitter in their dreaminess. "I certainly know.
Valentine's quite an addition to the social life of Hyde Park,
what's left of it. How did we ever get along without him. He's
so genial—he's so noisy, with those Scotch and Japanese imita-
tions, and that gravel voice. He drowns all conversation out.
Full of life! Oh, yes, he's full of it! And because you brought
him here, everybody thinks he's your special pal. He says so
himself. Only . . ."

"Only what?"

Tense and quiet, Asphalter asked, "Don't you know?" He became very pale.

"What should I know?"

"I took it for granted because your intelligence is so high— way off the continuum—that you knew something or suspected."

Something frightful was about to descend on him. Herzog nerved himself for it.

"Madeleine, you mean? I understand, of course, that by and by, because she's still a young woman, she must . . . she will."

"No, no," said Asphalter. "Not by and by." He blurted it out. "All the while."

Bellow was to have met us at the Sterns' house to decide our evening plans. He had said over leaf-burning that he wished to spend the evening with me, he realized that I had been in town twenty-four hours and we had hardly conversed. But when I returned from dinner with the Sterns he was not there. Instead, a message awaited us, asking us to join him for dinner at Station J.B.D., a restaurant at 1435 East Hyde Park. But we had already *had* dinner. I thought he had understood that that was why we had not gone with him to the cocktail party with Rosenberg and the French expert on Marxism.

Still, I could sit with him while he had *his* dinner, and for that purpose I dashed off to Station J.B.D., but he was not there, nor had the hostess seen him, nor did she expect him. She was a brisk, businesslike, blonde woman who became impatient with my repeated questions. I telephoned his apartment, but he was not there. Nor had he turned up at the Sterns. Clearly he wished to evade me. At that contest he was a sure winner, for Chicago was a very big meadow and Bellow an experienced woodchuck. I was a stranger on alien turf. I returned to the Sterns.

Frankly speaking, I said to the Sterns, I had an old friend in Chicago whom I had not seen in seven years, who often urged me to call if I came to town, and I now thought I'd do so, which I did. She invited me to a party. I accepted. Bellow was disappointing to me, this was the end, I would go to her party and drown my sorrow upon her breast, which I remembered.

But Stern would not surrender. He felt that a misunderstanding had occurred. Therefore he questioned his son, Chris, who had taken the message from Bellow, and who now supplied additional details: Bellow had said we were to meet him at Station J.B.D. *if we had not already had dinner;* Chris told him we *were* dining.

Bellow therefore went to dinner, but not to Station J.B.D. He never imagined, apparently, that I might just wish to sit and talk with him—I needn't eat. I think he did not think of himself as interesting to listen to if listening were an isolated act: to dine, drink, ride, walk, yes. But just to listen? He had written *Herzog* seventeen times; he would write *Humboldt's Gift* thirty times. That is to say, he didn't glitter off the top of his head. The very act of writing was compensation for one's being so otherwise commonplace. Men and women with golden tongues seldom write well, and Bellow knew I had met enough writers to know better than to race after them to watch them eat.

Even so, I went one last time to Station J.B.D., only to find the situation unchanged and the hostess ruder than ever. I returned to my car. I would find my way to my friend's party even in this unknown city. At the last moment, however, I changed direction and drove back past the Sterns' house, where I was pleased to see Bellow's car parked, and he within the house in the company of Harold Rosenberg. They were discussing either Tolstoy's story, "The Death of Ivan Ilyitch," or the social critic by that name.

I felt that my daughter and my subject ought to meet. Therefore I summoned Hester from above. In *Henderson the Rain King* Henderson names a sow "Hester." Now, meeting the real Hester, Bellow appeared not to approve of her, gazing upon her coldly, making her uncomfortable. She was barefoot, and she carried a long, green shawl serving her also as a kind of defense, shield, or armor, against his penetrating view. She wore a bright orange leotard. This was the period of the rising of American children against the war in Vietnam, and against related abuses. I thought that their rising was worth whatever cost.

Who was Bellow to Hester Harris, seventeen? Hester was a magnificent reader, she had read some of his work, and she was at that time perhaps more respectful than moved. He was not yet for her. In years afterward she would read him exceedingly well, finding in him many things I had missed. And she would remember feeling that he did not welcome children at the scene of adult conversation, whereupon, without a word, she wrapped her shawl ever more tightly about her, turned, and retreated upstairs to young people of more interest to her.

It was confusing to me that Bellow, who hated guns and war, was never associated with the protest against the war in Vietnam. Long lists of writers appeared in many advertisements in many places. Bellow's name was never there. Almost alone of his class or type he resisted the historic moment. From the beginning he had hated war, even the anti-Nazi war. He had stood or dangled alone with Joseph: "Steidler asked me how I was using my liberty. I answered that I was preparing myself spiritually, that I was willing to be a member of the Army, but not *part* of it." Joseph remains "insulated" from the war. Above all, he resists its rewards, precisely those rewards of license and self-indulgence so widely enjoyed during the anti-Vietnam period that one sometimes suspected that the war itself was forgotten. "Myself, I would rather die in the war than consume its benefits," says Joseph. "When I am called I shall go and make no protest. And, of course, I hope to survive. But I would rather be a victim than a beneficiary."

> And if after the hunt goes past
> And the double-barreled blast
> (Like war and pestilence
> And loss of common sense),
> If I can with confidence say
> That still for another day,
> Or even another year,
> I will be there for you, my dear,
> It will be because, though small
> As measured against the All,
> I have been so instinctively thorough
> About my crevice and burrow.

Bellow's coolness toward Hester may have been directed more toward me than toward her, the indulgent father teaching his daughter to skip school, dress in bright colors (but no shoes) and speed off to Chicago on Friday afternoon. The paradox of the comfortable radical enraged Bellow continually. He would not be one of those. Consider Valentine Gersbach: "But as soon as he slams the door of his Continental he begins to talk like Karl Marx. I heard him at the Auditorium with an audience of two thousand people. It was a symposium on desegregation, and he let loose a blast against the affluent society. That's how it is. If you've got a good job, about fifteen grand a year, and health insurance, and a retirement fund, and maybe some stock as well, why shouldn't you be a radical too?"[5] Certain intellectuals, he said, are "hedonists and really enjoy their revolutionary passions against a background of institutional safety."[6] I read this remark at a moment when I was certainly enjoying my own revolutionary passions at Purdue University—parading, marching, inciting, leading, demonstrating, speaking through a microphone—and it was going to cause me a good deal of difficulty. "They seem to have it both ways," Bellow wrote in an essay. "On the one hand these teachers, editors or culture-bureaucrats have absorbed the dislike of the modern classic writers for modern civilization. They are repelled by the effrontery of power and the degradation of the urban crowd. They have made the Waste Land outlook their own."[7] But, as Herzog perceives, the terrible danger lay in the fact that, for a variety of reasons, "it was easy for the Wastelanders to be assimilated to totalitarianism."

In politics, as in literature, Bellow followed his conviction. To stand alone might be painful, but not impossible. Lionel Trilling has described it with grace: "When, for example, a gifted novelist, Saul Bellow, tries through his Moses Herzog to question the prevailing negation of the old vision and to assert the value of the achieved and successful life, we respond with discomfort and embarrassment. And the more, no doubt, because we discern some discomfort and embarrassment on the part of Mr. Bellow himself, arising from the sufficiently accurate apprehension that in controverting the accepted attitude he lays himself open to the terrible charge of philistinism."[8]

It was necessary now to decide which party to go to, whether to go to the party to which Bellow and Rosenberg had been invited or to

5. *Herzog.*
6. In an interview in the New York *Times,* December 1, 1969.
7. "Cloister Culture," *The Best of "Speaking of Books,"* ed. Francis Brown (New York: Holt, Rinehart and Winston, 1969), p. 7.
8. "The Honest Soul and the Disintegrated Consciousness," *Sincerity and Authenticity* (Cambridge, Mass.: Harvard University Press, 1972), pp. 41–42.

attend the party to which my old friend had invited me. Bellow telephoned *his* party to learn its progress, asking many questions to establish the identities of people already there, people expected, people possible, and hanging up to think it all over. I telephoned my old friend at her party, asking whether I might bring two men with me (if, indeed, they chose hers above another—I had never been less my own master, I would explain it to her some time). I did not mention the names of my men. I did not wish to use Bellow's name for special favors, nor to trade upon Rosenberg's fame as a critic of art. She consulted her hostess, who accepted the idea of two unknown men.

Bellow and Rosenberg decided that my party was the one we ought to go to. I do not know their criteria. (As we shall see, going to my party may have been only a way of getting to theirs!) Perhaps Lake Shore Drive attracted them. Not so down on Lake Shore Jews as Susan said. We departed.

Bellow said we would reach the party more quickly if he drove. I gave him the key to my Falcon. Herzog's accident with his daughter, after their excursion to the aquarium, occurred in a Falcon. I reminded Bellow of this, urging him to drive with special care. I winced at the idea of my dying in Cook County Hospital, where my wife's father had died. "Herzog owned a Falcon?" Bellow politely asked. "I don't think so."

"He rented it," I said. "He was worried about his credentials and his dishevelment—don't you remember?—but the lady rented it to him anyhow, no questions asked."

"They'll rent to anybody," Bellow said.

Rosenberg talked of the early exhaustion or decline of American artists. I think he meant mainly painters, but he also shrewdly distinguished between factors governing the longevity of poets as opposed to novelists. I speculated from the back seat that Bellow was one of the few American novelists who had remained artistically alive in spite of acclaim: he never completed his work because he never completed his life, kept living it, kept groping, never saying *fini*, never moving to California nor sitting for his biographical portrait.

Rosenberg analyzed with insight and animation the problems Herbert Blau was then having as director of theater at Lincoln Center in New York. Bellow, for some reason, had an aversion to Blau's writing, although I had always thought of Blau's prose as powerful and distinguished. Bellow criticized Blau's *The Impossible Theater* for rallying "too much intellectual material to make a small point Blau could have made himself." For example, "Why call in Sartre to say something Blau can say just as well?" When I wrote something about Blau for Bellow's magazine *Anon*. I described him as "a professor of English." Bellow, as editor, wrote in the margin of my manuscript, "a language he doesn't know." On another occasion he said that Blau's prose was "like an elevator trying to move sideways." His unreason on the subject always baffled me. I began to wonder if he associated Blau with the whole unpleasant topic of my letter from France, in which I had named Blau as a potential subject for me of equal interest to Bellow.

Well, this was more like it. This was *it*—riding along with my biographee. Things at last were going right. Off to a party together, talking, rambling around from topic to topic, joking, gossiping, interrupting one another with opinions, expressing prejudices. And then, after the large party had reduced itself to a few persons, we would sit somewhere in a quiet place talking the dawn in. I imagined not only the night ahead, but long summers of green walking, long winters beside steam radiators. Three times a year, perhaps four, I would come up from Purdue to harvest the life, lore, legend, thought, and wisdom of Bellow, returning to Purdue to sort it out, write it down, codify it, alphabetize it, pack it tight on 3 × 5 cards, let it all shake down, all fall into place until, at last, unable to wait a moment longer, I would sit to write. Travel. Research. Necessary to interview many persons. Women. Bellow proceeded along the lake front to a high, elegant new building in the 3000-block, Lake Shore Drive. He parked my car, tipping the doorman for "keeping an eye on it," and we rose to the apartment of Hilda Solomon. Her husband, I heard, had been the architect of the building—easy work, compared to the creation of good biography, for a building need only imitate a plan, whereas the elements of biography are slippery, intangible, subject to endless interpretation.

We were greeted at the door by my old friend Naomi. She wore a striped jersey, black stockings upon sturdy, stocky legs, and a miniskirt—"No, Sammler changed that, it was a microskirt, a band of green across the thighs . . ." Sammler, sitting in the hospital with Angela, waiting for her father to die, asks her, ". . . do you think you should arrive in such a costume?"

"This skirt you mean?"

"It's very short. My opinion may be worthless, but it seems bad judgment to wear that kind of sexual kindergarten dress."

Impulsively we kissed, for we remembered each other with fondness, and soon Bellow and others were kissing, too, since, as it turned out, he had several acquaintances among the guests. I was pleased about this. It suggested how naturally his environment was mine, how certainly I belonged, how highly qualified I was to be his biographer—see how naturally I had stepped into his Chicago circle, leading *him* to *his* old friends. In *my* automobile. (He driving.)

Soon I was engaged in conversation with Zita Cogan, who had attended high school with Bellow. What high school? She mentioned the name. I didn't quite catch it. Research.

Herzog, in 1934, "was class orator at the McKinley High School, his text taken from Emerson." (Allbee, the anti-Semite, bitter Gentile of *The Victim*, laments his displacement by the Jews: "It may not strike you as it struck me, but I go into the library once in a while, to look around, and last week I saw a book about Thoreau and Emerson by a man named Lipschitz.")

Bellow, in 1934, was in his nineteenth year. Born in 1915. I would become an expert at subtracting fifteen from any year. But it wasn't McKinley, it was Tuley, where he belonged to the Debating Club with Isaac Rosenfeld. "It is late afternoon, a spring day, and the Tuley Debating Club is meeting on the second floor of the old building since destroyed by fire. The black street doors are open, the skate wheels are buzzing on the hollow concrete, and the handballs strike the walls with a taut puncturing sound. Upstairs, I hold the gavel. Isaac rises and asks for the floor. He has a round face, somewhat pale, glasses, and his light hair is combed back with earnestness and maturity. He is wearing short pants. His subject is *The World as Will and Idea*, and he speaks with perfect authority. He is very serious. He has read Schopenhauer."[9]

Twenty years later I knew Rosenfeld in Minneapolis. Then almost instantly he was dead. How shall I track down the Class of 1934 Tuley High? How has this Zita Cogan spent these thirty-three years since graduation day? Who was she to Bellow? Was she a casual acquaintance, simple school chum? Or was she the intensest lover of his life? If the latter, I am hot on the trail. I suppose I could ask. But

9. "Isaac Rosenfeld," *Partisan Review*, Fall 1956, p. 565.

would she answer? Are you now or have you ever been the mistress of my biographical subject?

And this was only one more or less accidental evening's encounter in Chicago. Think of the two hundred other places Bellow has lived, or so he told Jane Howard of *Life*, who made a point in her article of having shared with Bellow the privacy of his apartment—"But in private he is different. At home, in his five-room South Side Chicago apartment, he is as eager a host as a lonely child at his own birthday party."[10] Not very good writing. How does Jane Howard know how her moment of privacy with Bellow stacks up against the rest of his life? This leaves the biographer with the questions, "Who was Jane Howard? What was she to Bellow? Where did she stand in his affection when compared to Zita Cogan?" Jane Howard wrote a book called *Please Touch* in which she tells of other hours all around the country, visiting installations of the "human potential movement," touching, feeling, massaging, back-rubbing, counseling, "co-counseling," having peak experiences, therapy, pretending to have a baby, pretending to be a fish, bathing nude with strangers, sending and receiving I-messages, U-messages, overcoming shyness, eyeballing crotches—"Later Dick and Maxine submitted to having their crotches eyeballed. Bindrim said he was only sorry there wasn't time for all of us to have this experience."[11] What really went on between Bellow and Jane in his apartment? She says he showed her "the medal he got from the French government." Charlie Citrine received such a medal. "'The Legion of Honor. I'm a knight, a *chevalier*,'" Charlie exults. But Bellow is slightly embarrassed by Citrine's bourgeois joy, and he causes Humboldt to send him a postcard: "'*Shoveleer! Your name is now lesion.*'" It was all too foolish, these prizes, these validations, and after a hundred pages Bellow punctured the prize: "Actually, the medal is a kind of phony. Major decorations are red, not green. They gave me the sort of thing they give to pig-breeders and to people who improve the garbage cans. A Frenchman told me last year that my green ribbon must be the lowest rank of the Legion of Honor. In fact he had never actually seen a green ribbon before." An American cop has his own opinion: "That? I wouldn't tie it on a chicken leg."

10. "Mr. Bellow Considers His Planet," *Life*, April 3, 1970, p. 58.
11. (New York: McGraw-Hill, 1970), p. 96.

Thing led to thing. How could I ever stop it? Research was end-less, theories were infinite, people were widely dispersed, people were dead, or people just weren't talking. Bellow had drifted from sight. I found him sitting with Toby Harris. I heard that they, too, were longtime friends, as I might have guessed when I saw for my-self how affectionately her hand lingered upon him as they talked. Please touch.

Irving Harris joined us. Toby's husband. He was a psychiatrist, au-thor of a book called *The Promised Seed*. He seemed to me to be a man of gentleness, good humor, and—to judge by his book, which I afterward read—wisdom or modesty, accepting his own theories tentatively, giving the reader generous quantities of self-confuting information.

In *The Promised Seed* he has made a study of "eminent" men, male achievers, including many literary men, to seek distinctions, if any, between first sons and later sons. "It is clear . . . that it is one thing to be humanized or socialized principally by a parent, and an-other thing to be done so principally by a sibling or a peer."[12] After we had talked awhile he said, "I've been listening to your remarks on various subjects. You have a strong interest in the underdog, and in justice. I think by a ratio of 70 to 30 that you are a later son."

I was sorry to disappoint him. I am a first son. Bellow is a later son. (Third son, fourth child, he has been quoted by Stern as saying, "All I started out to do was show up my brothers. I didn't have to go this far."[13]) Theoretically, first sons receive the finer part of parental devotion, leading them to believe that the world, on the whole, is made for *them*. Later sons know better. First sons are more likely to be "responsive to an inner moral authority." Later sons, however, "speak more of a morality derived from social norms." First sons give commands and later sons follow them.

First sons tend to believe in an orderly universe, and seek to ex-plain it. Bellow has tendencies that way, but when his characters set out to explain it they turn somewhat comic.

First sons think of themselves as heroic. Bellow is antiheroic. First sons are optimists—not surprising, given their illusions of an orderly universe commanded by their heroic selves. But Bellow is an

12. (New York: Free Press, 1964), p. 10.
13. "Bellow's Gift," *New York Times Magazine*, November 21, 1976, p. 42.

optimist, possibly because of his frequently successful resistance to the domination or command of his older brothers.

On the night of my meeting with Dr. Harris I *felt* very much like a later son—Bellow's younger brother, by seven years. It was Bellow, after all, who had decided which party we would go to, he who took the wheel and drove us to it, and he who, as we shall see, undertook even to direct the kid brother's romantic life, although I was almost at the end of my forty-fifth year.

Joseph, Augie, Henderson, Herzog, Charlie Citrine—all, all are later sons overwhelmed by older brothers. Dr. Harris's theory admits ambiguities, but Bellow's central character, book to book, cuts through uncontradicted by conflicting data. Following the struggle, we see Bellow's true heart, the terrible forces of life he would rout if he could. This is what he purely stands for. Here is his politics. Older brothers are rich, encouraging the dependence of the later son. They offer lavish material rewards for obedience and conformity. They tempt their younger brother, exploiting him as they exploit everyone else; they *use* him. They rescue him from difficulties brought down upon himself by his own passionate art or intellect, and thereby they enjoy vindication. They are "the person who 'knows-the-world-for-what-it-is.'"

Older brothers—first sons in Dr. Harris's nomenclature—show contempt for mere powerless literary or artistic persons. They themselves are known to City Hall, Washington. Shura Herzog rates a motorcycle escort, but when Herzog weeps at the funeral to which they were escorted brother Shura scolded him: "Don't carry on like a goddamn immigrant." First sons are well adjusted to America. "Your brothers have done okay, right here in this town," but Herzog himself, although "you can look up his name in the library . . . has no money in the bank." Herzog speaks of "a strange division of functions that I sense, in which I am the specialist in . . . in spiritual self-awareness; or emotionalism; or ideas; or nonsense. Perhaps of no real use or relevance except to keep alive primordial feelings of a certain sort. He [brother Will] mixes grout to pump into these new high-risers all over town. He has to be political, and deal, and wangle and pay off and figure tax angles." "All this fucking art!" says brother Julius Citrine. "I never understood the play you wrote. I went away in the second act."

Older brothers want their younger brother to marry rich; not for love—a theme sounded in at least three novels. But women are ir- relevant to the he-man's world of owning, killing, plundering, gorg- ing, and wasting. Older brothers are patriotic, but they hide their money in foreign banks. They are pious, cruel, brutal, and senti- mental—"sentiment and brutality—never one without the other, like fossils and oil," moans Herzog. They love death. They are fat and slothful, and their breasts are womanlike. They will *buy* Charlie Citrine if they must, to tutor their children: "My kids ought to learn a foreign language, have a little culture." They are callous, aesthetically zero, denying history, denying their own family past for which they have no pragmatic use.

"My brother Amos, who is my senior by twelve years, is a wealthy man," Joseph tells us in *Dangling Man*, Bellow's first book, first leg of the literary journey from innocence to wholeness. "The family is very proud of him, and he, in turn, has been a reliable son, very much alive to his duties. Toward me he took a protective attitude at first, but he soon gave up, confessing that he did not know what I was after. He was hurt when I became a radical, relieved when he assured himself I was one no longer. He was disappointed when I married Iva. His own wife, Dolly, had a rich father. He had urged me to follow his example and marry a wealthy woman." Amos presses money on Joseph, boasts of his own income, and urges Joseph to en- ter military service. When, at last, Joseph finally joins the army, Amos would become, if he could, beneficiary of that action: "Amos, when I spoke to him yesterday, asked me to have lunch with him at his club. I told him I was going to be busy. I knew he would have introduced me to his friends as 'my brother who is going into the Army,' and would thereafter be known as a man who was 'in it.'"

Sixty years old, meeting his brother Sam in Israel, Bellow wrote of that encounter as if time, ripeness, mellowness, had settled all the old scores, whatever they might have been. But perhaps not. When one has unhappy things to say one says it in fiction, which brothers of a certain kind are unlikely to penetrate. At any rate, the meeting in Israel offers almost the only lines of Bellow in which brothers confront without conflict or passion: "My brother Sam, who is visit- ing Jerusalem with his wife, astonishes me: he turns up at my door. In the States this would never happen. We live at opposite ends of

Chicago and make appointments on the telephone for lunch or dinner. Our routines take us in different directions. So it must be thirty years or more since we faced each other at leisure on an ordinary morning. We are silently amused. My brother's smile is jaunty and exceptionally communicative. We look at each other. Except for the eyes, we are entirely changed. We have mainly this brown-eyed evidence that there is an age-free essence in each of us, unaltered. The rest is wrinkles. And why shouldn't we smile?"[14]

Suddenly something revealed itself which I have never been able to explain. Bellow, it appeared, had made arrangements with Irving and Toby Harris to leave the party with them. How could they have done that? I had been *sitting* with them. I had heard every word they said. It was some secret Chicago language I had not yet learned, and I was stung to feel that once again I was to be deprived of Bellow. Always a small mystery—indigestion, bad telephone signals—and now the Harrises carrying him off, having communicated with him furtively.

Except, of course, my old friend Naomi was here in her microskirt. Bellow said afterward that this *was* his plan—an evening with a woman so beautiful and so talented as Naomi was a treat. He wanted me to have it. She and I had instantly resumed our friendship. Speech and feeling flowed easily between us as if we had never been out of each other's sight. Over the years she had sent me some of her poetry, her reputation had advanced, and now she was writing a novel about a revolution in Latin America. At thirty-six years old she was gaining a confidence in herself she had not had before, it increased with her beauty, she was breaking through to herself; she had divorced a rich husband and carried forward a love affair with an Italian, though that ended in futility because of the awkwardness of the divorce laws of Italy. Life was wonderfully sufficient for her now without either husband or lovers. This I gathered as we talked. Philosophically she said, "My cards are on the table: no more complications," and at another moment, "Sex without love is a crime."

Bellow, Rosenberg, and the Harrises (Irving and Toby) offered many farewells at the door, and disappeared into the night. The party was suddenly reduced in size. Eight persons remained—"just

14. "Reflections," *The New Yorker*, July 19, 1976, p. 54.

the family," someone said. If family, very distant, for I had never met any of them before except Naomi.

Whatever Bellow's plans for me might have been they were not necessarily shared by Naomi. She was not about to be dragged through the streets at all hours of the night. On the contrary, she had a train to catch. She was living these days—or was temporarily housed, in the manner of poets—in the Indiana dunes, many miles away. I offered to drive her to the railroad station. Saying good-bye to our family, we went down to my Falcon.

Of course she assumed I knew where the railroad station was. I thought I had received good instructions before leaving the party, but apparently I had not. I was lost. Naomi's curiosity was aroused —where was I going? I was not certain. Indeed, I did not know at all. She grew cross. Even if we found the railroad station now, she said, we would be too late for the train, we must try for the South Side instead—did I know where the South Side was? The lake, I said, is always east. We were soon on a highway or freeway or parkway, beside a body of water I'd have called Lakeside Drive if I'd been given Chicago to invent, but she cried no, get off, it was all wrong, get into the other lane. "Aim for the exit!" she called, which we missed, though she had urged it upon me with great force. "You've done it," she wailed.

We had now committed ourselves irrevocably, she said, to the long drive to the Indiana dunes. We had missed all trains out of Chicago, and all exits from this highway. Yet she could not be sure. She had only her sunglasses with her. My own eyes had been distressed since yesterday, and they burned now with the smoke of her cigarettes and the onset of fatigue. I knew old sensations, night, tobacco, a long drive, questions of chance and intention, ambiguities, complicated always by deep regrets, strong alternatives, accusations: she said I had dumped Bellow for her.

Not true. Here I was, perfectly free, riding through the long night with a woman of the world, an international poet, wishing I were with Bellow, whom I had come to Chicago to see. "(What a lot of romances! thought Herzog. One after another. Were those my real career?)" "His achievements were not only scholarly but sexual." Or wishing at least that I were back in the Sterns' house where my daughter, my chaperone, more or less expected me, who would be surprised and shocked to think of my having left Chicago without her; having left, indeed, the whole State of Illinois, careening now across the Indiana dunes.

Did Naomi care to go to a bar? Yes. She had given up husbands and lovers, but not a drink now and then. She said I might stay the night at her cabin. She explained the arrangement of the beds. I could have my own personal bed. We did not find a bar. I did not really look for one. I thought a bar would complicate my life in ways a coffee shop would not, and we stopped for coffee at a roadside restaurant where we squinted with burning eyes into the fluorescent lighting, the air was greased, the silence of weariness hung at two o'clock mingling with the smoke of broiling and the fumes and miasma of the night. I had not quite been here in years. I thought I had gone forward, but I was the same as ever. Unchanged. I seemed to hear on the jukebox songs of 1944. Naomi said, "This is sounding like a movie."

I drove her to the railroad station somewhere in the dunes where she had parked her car. The place had the word "Grove" in it. One other car was parked there—someone detained in Chicago, arrested, dead, sick, drunk, blissful at a rendezvous, working all night at the office. I waited to see that Naomi's motor was well begun, and I drove back toward Chicago, wishing I had more keenly observed our coming, once or twice turning to recover my direction, and the hour approaching three. I was almost alone on the Indiana Tollway. I had wasted quantities of time and energy, diminished myself in my own eyes, fool who had come all this distance to see Bellow and then let him get away like that. I was doomed to a miserable day tomorrow without even a compensating memory of having foolishly but gloriously dragged myself through the dunes all night. I would awaken tomorrow with gravel in my eyes, if indeed I found my way back to Chicago in the first place. Rain began. I approached spectacular tongues of flame lighting the sky above the smokestacks of Gary.

Suddenly, in Chicago, the traffic became heavy, whether people returning late or rising early I did not know, nor where I was, North or South. On the South Side, crossing Fifty-first Street, traveling toward Kimbark, I think, the streets teemed with black people, lights ablaze, all things active, as if it were day. Somewhere on Fifty-first Street, "under the el," as I recall, Herzog first saw Daisy, who became his wife.

SURPRISINGLY, after a brief sleep, I awoke marvelously refreshed, forthright, decisive, and positive. My eyes by a miracle had perfectly recovered. I showered, went down to breakfast, and soon called Bellow, who answered in a prompt and friendly manner. I said I hoped we could meet today, I had "formulated" certain remarks I wished to address to him. "I want to end the strain," I said.

"Yes," he said, "neither of us can afford it." I hadn't known he was under any. However, he said, he could not be available until 4:30 in the afternoon, it was Sunday, and he was obliged to take "the kid" to the zoo. I had always thought the phrase "the kid" in Bellow's writing was meant as a humorous echo of popular diction; now I heard his own use of it. Thereafter, reading Bellow, whenever I came upon the phrase, as I often did, I was gently reminded once more that he was not so much philosopher as storyteller, telling his own self-involved tale, not only artist but pained and laughing participant, victim of Humanitis.

I said I would be delighted to accompany him and Daniel to the zoo. But if Daniel thought me an intruder I would not go. Or was I giving too much power of decision to a three-year-old child? Bellow said he understood these alternatives. He would arrange his day. It depended on the weather, rain was threatening, he'd watch the weather and telephone me "in a little while." We rang off.

Fool! One more failed conversation! Bellow's "little while" might be tomorrow or next year or never. In my new alertness I could easily see this as one more woodchuck trick. But in a few minutes Hester came running to summon me from brushing my teeth—Bellow on the telephone. I threw down my toothbrush.

Greetings again.

Could I come to see him now?

Yes, I could leave in four minutes, and he gave me elaborate directions for finding his door once I had found his building, for his door had no name on it, and I must be sure to rap hard, he might be shaving.

It was a tall building, called the Cloisters, overlooking a field or park where men were playing soccer. I rapped hard. He answered the door bare-chested, excused himself, and returned to the bathroom. He was shaving. I thought (then or now) of Willie Mays, the wonderful baseball player, who had once kept me waiting for an hour in his besieged house in San Francisco while he disappeared "just to stick the bottle in the baby's mouth." Of Ernie Banks, eluding me in Chicago; of Robert Frost hiding. Why didn't they just give me the go-ahead? *Carte blanche.* In the end I wrote them up with love. What secrets were they afraid of my giving away? Couldn't they see that if I was a spy I was a *friendly* spy? In this connection I had brought with me for our conversation a scrap of paper torn from the *New York Review of Books* stacked at the Sterns. Elizabeth Hardwick was speculating on the Kennedy family's selection of a biographer for the late president: "It would be untrue to say that [Manchester's] choice by the Kennedy family is a puzzle: it is not in the least. Few people with power and money realize that the eulogist blackens more reputations than the liar. The only hope for public figures, if they would be remembered as a genuine presence, is to be observed, perhaps almost surreptitiously, by another genuine person who might one day write down his thoughts."[15]

Bellow soon returned to the living room, pulling on his shirt. I was impressed by the breadth and the depth of his gray-haired chest—he was not so slender as I had thought, but stockier, heftier through the middle. We sat on facing chairs. He seemed to slouch, hiding. Frost had slouched. Or perhaps it was I who slouched. I remember only the sense of slouching. During our conversation the phone rang twice, and he spoke briefly. One of the callers was Bonne Amie, whom I had met in March.

I formally began. I was shy, I said, about speaking of ourselves as if we were Johnson and Boswell, but I did think he was as shrewd an observer of our age as Johnson was of his. I hoped, therefore, that he would make things easy for me to trail him around for fifteen or twenty days a year for the next few years—I was right there at Purdue, a few hours away, I could come and go with fair freedom, I was already a master of the Indiana Tollway. For those fifteen or twenty days a year I would keep an elaborate journal of everything that was said and every place we went and every presence there. I would be eavesdropping on him. I would dog his steps, "perhaps almost surreptitiously," as in Hardwick. I read him the passage from Hardwick.

On the other hand, I said, if he opposed my surreptitiously follow-

15. "The Death of a President," *New York Review of Books*, April 20, 1967.

ing him about during the years ahead he should certainly say so *now*, and relieve the strain on me.

Surprising to me, Bellow asked, "How will that relieve the strain on you?"

"Why," said I, unaware of all that he had missed in me, "I'll *stop*. Just tell me to stop and I'll promise to stop and never write a word about you as long as I live, though I would certainly hope we'd continue to be friends."

Bellow seemed to see something now he had not seen before. He saw that I had misunderstood something. I *was* free. I was free to write about him as I pleased. How could he stop me? But he saw that he, too, had misunderstood something: that I would not write about him without his permission, his cooperation, his knowledge, that I was in some way—here I use nice phrasing from his writing—"oddly faithful to things you learned as a boy,"[16] asking permission not because I needed permission but because I *wanted* it, because I was a writer, not a spy; because I was a writer, not a gossip-columnist; because I was a writer, not an undercover reporter; because between a writer and his subject not only permission must pass but trust must pass, and confidence, and after enough time and sympathetic inquiry came love.

Bellow's own worthiness had looked bad there for a moment against my boyish purity: not I, but he, imagined my working without his consent. He saw me wrong (not surprising) as that lickety-split professional whom he had first met roaring along in a rented car from Frost to Tivoli to New York, appearing again in Chicago nearly five years later hot on the trail of a first baseman, "shooting up and down the general area west of the Rockies." My own words, after all. Wheeler-dealer, flying around the world on Henry Luce's expense account, $60,000 in securities untouched by human hands, now here, now there, whipping off a letter from France. Full of projects. "When I'm in your presence," I said, "I'm never quite myself. I seem to play a role. Sometimes I think you force me into it."

"Now *Stern*," he deftly replied, "Stern couldn't write about me because as a writer he couldn't *subordinate* himself to me."

16. "Distractions of a Fiction Writer," *The Living Novel*, ed. Granville Hicks (New York: Macmillan Co., 1957).

Johnson was an aggressive advocate of subordination, loved the word, and used it often. "I think you're wrong," I said, "I think Stern thinks of you as being in a class by yourself." Perhaps my reply was a way of speaking of myself by speaking of Stern. "Maybe he could subordinate himself. Maybe he couldn't. We wouldn't know until he tried, would we?"

Bellow spoke along lines I think he had been formulating yesterday among the burning leaves: Johnson is dead. Such an age is past. Literature, in Johnson's time, existed, for better or for worse, at the center of thought of influential society; Johnson in turn at the center of literature. The English-speaking literate world, not more nor less than educated London, sought from Samuel Johnson the answers to things. But now, in our time, literature was removed from the active center of things. To be heard, literary people were required to scramble for attention, to "compete," and Bellow refused to do this. He would not seek publicity. He could not worry about his "image"—his image must worry about itself. "Publicity," said he, "is a low form of art." Moreover, biography is for the man who is finished—unless, of course, he is merely seeking publicity. "I'm not finished, not done, not *fini*. I'm still groping."

Now, said Bellow, regarding this other matter: "Prudence is important, but it doesn't really concern me. I don't care about your eavesdropping or bugging me—that's in your imagination. When we talk I become absorbed in the conversation, and I forget that you're eavesdropping." He insisted that he had not in any way been "evading" me this weekend. He hadn't known I was coming to Chicago, he hadn't known the Harrises were to be at the party. "Any sense that you have that I'm resisting you is more in your imagination than in reality." Saturday afternoon, for example, he had been terribly distracted by Susan with a handful of bills when he had gone to pick up Daniel.

As for last night, he had suspected that I would find my old friend Naomi more pleasing than he. It was the choice he himself would have made. He was not fleeing from me but serving me: an evening with *him* I might have any time, but an evening with a woman so talented, so intelligent as Naomi ought to be seized when it came. Therefore he engaged Irving and Toby Harris's wheels for himself and Rosenberg. "I took the instantaneous view," said Bellow, "that she ought to be amused, I knew that you were on the spot for the job," he wished me to have a clear field and a free vehicle.

"You are the soul of kindness," I said. "It didn't work out. I'd rather have been listening to you."

Bellow was interested in the mechanics of my journal, into which I would put all this surreptitious eavesdropping. I told him that I had recently had installed in my house in San Francisco a fireproof vault where I could confidentially keep anything I wrote about him or anybody else. I was in no hurry to publish. I could take years. Ten, fifteen years. More. Longer. Who knows? Boswell took twenty-eight years between the day he met Johnson and the day the *Life* was published. Was there something Bellow especially feared? Sexual scandal?

"Who could reveal more than I already have about *that*?" he asked. "I have no fears about anything. You can write anything you want about me."

That sounded recklessly *carte blanche*. At any rate, it was good to hear, a delayed answer to my letter written to him fifteen months before, from France. My whole body was pleased with his reply. I felt that I had won something. I took it as encouragement. It was all I ever needed and all I ever got. It gave me the spirit to work ahead, but not too fast.

We descended. As we alighted from the elevator we met an older man and woman whom Bellow knew. They were Professor and Mrs. Blair. Blair's name leaped at me off the spines of many books . . . Mark Twain . . . *Native American Humor* . . . I felt myself to be a native American humorist, and so was he. He said to Bellow, "We saw that you'd moved in. When will the orgies begin?" He was feeble, however. Stern told me he had almost died of a disease that "ate up his corpuscles." But a decade later he was about as ever.

Bellow and I walked. He had some destination. As we walked, we saw a man across the street with two dogs, and Bellow hailed him, for they were acquainted, calling, "You appear to be meditating." The man replied no, he was only waiting for the dogs to "go."

Next, a lovely lady in a foreign car swept past, and without stopping, but slightly slowing, thrust her head from the window, greeted Bellow, and continued to gaze, her eyes trained questioningly upon him, magnetically focused, her head swiveling amazingly in spite of her automobile's carrying her away. I asked him who she was. I praised her beauty. He did not recall her name, he said. Years later it occurred to me that we were perhaps walking to her house, that she expected him—that she was the second telephone caller—that she had begun to worry about his delay, that she was keeping breakfast warm in the oven while touring the streets in search of her promised guest.

Soon, anyhow, we stood in someone's courtyard; and clearly we were parting. He did not offer to tell me why he was here or who was within—withholding vital information from his biographer. I could write anything I wanted about him, but I had to find it out first. He said, "Lock your vault from your wife."

Chapter Five

I FELT that the air had cleared between us. He understood my procedure. I was free to go ahead without the guilt of surreptitiousness. But whether the air had really cleared I did not fully know. Perhaps it had never been unclear, except in my imagination—Bellow had said as much. But could I believe him?

During that fall term at Purdue I was "teaching" Bellow's first book, his novel *Dangling Man* (1944), to a class called "The Art of Prose Composition." Our little red Signet edition advertised itself as being "by the celebrated author of *Herzog*." I had read *Dangling Man* when I was as young as its hero. I was at that time writing my own book of military dangling. I grew up with Joseph, and with his successors as they came along. Of course! Because in some ways their lives were mine. After Joseph came Asa, Augie, Henderson, Tommy, Moses, Bummidge, Sammler, Citrine.

Now I was starting all through Bellow's books again. It was the year 1967, and our students were entering a period of historic distraction. The question was Vietnam, but their generation was not about to dangle, like Joseph, nor to go obediently to war, as Joseph's generation had gone. Not even to please brother Amos. During the period of Vietnam I was baffled by Bellow's dangling, I wished he would stop, I wanted him to come out against Johnson, Nixon, but I was able to see afterward that his dangling was his optimism, his bet upon the future, his balance, his perspective, his positing civilized life even beyond the degradation of Vietnam, as Joseph had posited life outliving Nazism.

Bellow was twenty-eight when *Dangling Man* was published. The book is not even precocious. It is frail, straightforward, digressive, amusing, in the style of a young man's journal. Hesitant. Unconfident. "I think that when I wrote those early books I was timid. I still felt the incredible effrontery of announcing myself to the world (in part I mean the WASP world) as a writer and an artist. I had to touch a great many bases, demonstrate my abilities, pay my respects to formal requirements. In short, I was afraid to let myself go."[1] Bellow tells us that his good friend John Berryman called those "early" books (*Dangling Man* and *The Victim*) "two small and correct books. He did not care for them."[2]

In *Dangling Man* every sentence is grammatically formal, proper, and complete. None of those fragments which characterize his later style. Which give his later style pace and speed. (Which I sometimes think is a kind of laziness.) Now and again, in *Dangling Man*, a passage seems to be about to rise into the air by elation, the author is discovering the joys and the pleasures of liberation; but for the moment he has dared enough, and he gently returns to earth.

One of the interesting things about "the celebrated author of *Herzog*" was that he had not always been. The uncelebrated author of *Dangling Man* was one of a great many young men and women starting out in writing during World War II without much indication whether this was the beginning or the end of writing, or how one confidently went about it, or where it might lead, or what the pleasures and the penalties might be, or what its real relationship was to money, love, livelihood, universities, philosophy, and social reform. What would it do to one's own mind? Bellow and hundreds of other young men and women milled at the starting line for the great marathon.

YOU HAVE read the book. Now see the author. I went again to Chicago in late December, once more with Hester turned seventeen, with Josephine her mother (my wife), with our friend Herbert Blau whose prose style Bellow had found wanting, and with Blau's daughter, Tara, sixteen. Tara's purpose in traveling to Chicago was to be interviewed for admission by the University of Chicago. She at-

---

1. "Saul Bellow: An Interview," *The Paris Review*, Winter 1966, p. 55.
2. Foreword to John Berryman's *Recovery* (New York: Farrar, Straus and Giroux, 1973), p. ix.

tended Cornell instead. Blau's plan was to deliver an address before a meeting of the annual convention of the Modern Language Association. My own plan was to see Bellow, which occurred quite easily, magically, without hitch, delay, confusion, or misunderstanding, somehow simply by Blau's speaking on the telephone (one call) with Stern—we would all dine at seven.

FIRST TO the Palmer House. There Charlie Citrine met Renata by appointment and Naomi Lutz by accident. Charlie had taken a room at conference rates, but he had some difficulty with the "sofa bed. . . . As soon as I saw this object I knew it would defeat me. I was sure I would never be able to get it open. Once anticipated this challenge would not leave my head. I had to meet it at once. The trapezoid foam-rubber bolsters weighed nothing. I pushed them away and pulled off the fitted spread. The sheets under it were perfectly clean. Then I knelt and groped under the sofa frame for a lever. Renata watched silent as my face grew tight and reddened. I crouched and pulled, furious with manufacturers who made such junk, and with the management for taking money from afternoon conferees and crucifying them in spirit. 'This thing is like an IQ test,' I said. 'So?' 'I'm flunking.'"

In the corridors among the afternoon conferees, standing with my back to a wall, strolling, listening, peering at nameplates, I seemed to see everyone I had known since first I took up life in an English Department. I shook hands with Henry Nash Smith, Leo Marx, Eric Solomon, Kay House, Victor Harris, Jules Chametzky, Jules Markels, Mary Shumway, Sam Monk, J. C. Levinson, and Leo Hamalian and a whole roomful of people from the City University of New York. Everyone I shook hands with introduced me to someone else whose name I did not catch, and many people said how awful it was, pretending to despise it.

True, the annual meeting of the Modern Language Association was a paradox. It was as if members of the American Automobile Association were to walk. The MLA convened to transact the business of a humane enterprise: the teaching of language and literature. But nothing was so fervently read at MLA as the airplane timetables people carried at all times and unfolded and read while my friend Herbert Blau delivered a learned paper upon which he had labored very hard. Not every paper-giver labored hard, if at all. Their objective was not to labor, but to be named as a participant, and thereby to inflate their claims to professional advancement. Every banquet room was in flux, coming and going, rising and rushing, trying to talk above the sound of the legitimate proceedings. Manners were as bad as manners at any political convention, and with less excuse.

Here were hundreds of people from departments of English in every state. Their basic work was the actual lovely labor of reading poems or books, but their consuming work was the bureaucratic labor of seeking advancement for themselves, for their institutions, and of interviewing and appraising candidates bred like them on poems and books. Because there were so many of us, and the country so big, the study of pleasing literature had ended in the proliferation of specialties. Nobody knew what anybody else was doing. "Scholars and critics," Bellow has written, "are often curiously like property owners. They have their lots surveyed. Here the property begins and there it ends. . . . For every poet now there are a hundred custodians and doctors of literature, and dozens of undertakers measuring away at coffins."[3]

But the irony was never really lost upon the convention itself. If the artist winced with discomfort, so did the scholar when the scholar was sensitive—"how quickly the visions of genius become the canned goods of the intellectual."[4] For myself, I knew that everything I had done as student and as teacher to satisfy the standards of the MLA had been good for me. My head was improved. Like Herzog, "set apart from daily labor for greater achievements," I could not have lived any other way, I could not have been an editor, agent, or fast writer. Almost alone, this profession granted me my brooding. Somewhere in the Palmer House I encountered Professor Samuel Monk. He had been much respected at Minnesota during my time there, and before, and after, and he said to me, "I'm surprised that you remember me." Who was I to forget Sam Monk—I who can remember the name of every teacher I have had since kindergarten? "Sam Monk is not memorable to himself," Bellow said afterward. Often the professor of literature seems to have forgotten what many of them may never have feelingly known, that literature is created in stress, yearning, and memory; on the whole, in Amer-

3. "Distractions of a Fiction Writer," *The Living Novel*, ed. Granville Hicks (New York: Macmillan Co., 1957), p. 16.
4. *Herzog*.

ica, by poor boys like Bellow or other eccentric outcast types, not necessarily poor, like Henry James.

Max Bluestone joined me. Bluestone, Blau, Bellow, Boswell. Bluestone was one to whom the profession had taught absolute precision. He was a professor at the University of Massachusetts in Boston, warrior against that bureaucracy of which the massed conglomeration of the MLA was the visible expression. He fought for private rights within the machine. Truest teacher of English, he came linguistically to issues, his primary sense his ear, detecting baseness, hollowness, the flawed argument, hypocrisy, meanness, chicanery, distortion or lying public or private by his perception of the word itself. During the early years of our friendship I sometimes thought he was *hung up* on words. Then I saw how right a prophet he was. By etymology he tracked the meaning of the mind that wagged the tongue. He computed. He was the master, in Frost's phrase, of "feats of association." We left the Palmer House by taxicab.

Our party assembled at a Chinese restaurant on 63rd Street, near Dorchester, I believe, on the South Side. I think this restaurant was a favorite of the Sterns, who had taken me there April 5, 1961. The Sterns arrived with Paul Fussell, of Rutgers, and Fussell's wife, whose name I never learned; and with Bellow and his companion, a woman of twenty-five (I guessed or was told) named or called Stat or Stats or Stap or Staps. She may have been the model for Citrine's friend Demmie, who "taught Latin at the Washington Irving School . . . had blue eyes with clean whites and an upturned nose that confronted you almost as expressively and urgently as the eyes. The length of her front teeth kept her mouth slightly open. . . . Hers was the sort of face you might have seen in a Conestoga wagon a century ago, a pioneer face, a very white sort of face. . . . In a cocktail crowd, where I met her, I could scarcely understand what she was saying, for she muttered in the incomprehensible fashionable Eastern lockjaw manner." In my own journal I had written: "She is not beautiful, but she has a saucy face, an upturned nose, short straight hair, fitting, for me, the stereotype in face of a saucy barmaid. But she is educated, intelligent, Episcopalian, with an engaging habit, either because of her bronchial cough, or for another reason, of suddenly blurting her speech as if she's trying to beat the coughing."

In any case, a most enticing person so scantily dressed as to give the appearance of one who lacked confidence in her mind. But her mind was superb, whether she knew it or not. She was a catcher in the rye, teacher in a private school in New York, where she was always exhausted, but in spite of many temptations to quit her job she could not do so: she felt that quitting would be desertion, abandoning her "tens" and "twelves" to the "cruelty" of the nuns. She could neither happily stop nor happily continue. She had discussed this dilemma with Bellow, who had urged her to resign, but his suggestion only erected in her mind certain questions about Bellow himself: what kind of man could it be who advocated abandoning helpless children to nuns?

We sat at several tables formed to make one. I sat first to Josephine's left, but that was absurd—why come all the way to Chicago to sit beside my wife?—and she urged me to sit beside Bellow. "Go for the tidbits," said Stern to me, and I took the place beside Bellow.

Well, this was more like it. This was *it*—sitting at table with my biographee. Off to dinner together, discussing the menu, talking about his books, surveying other diners. Josephine had never met Bellow, and for some time she had expressed the desire not to do so: if I were to write a biography of him she preferred to remain aloof, as a means of remaining my good clear-eyed critic. She would read him. She had read his books as they were offered, but none with enthusiasm until his latest, *Herzog*, whose hero, however, my wife condemned for his always coming at women with a judgment of their bodies. By such a standard a woman has achieved her moment of highest value at the age of Miss Stat (let us call her that), sitting coughing there. But Josephine's idea of herself was that she had not gone downhill but *improved* since her own age twenty-five. Except in the story "Leaving the Yellow House," Josephine felt, Bellow had never created women of magnitude: never a Rose of Sharon, Ma, or Elisa Allen as in Steinbeck; no Bundren women, no Temple Drake, no Dilsey, as in Faulkner; no Catherine Barkley, no Pilar, no Lady Brett Ashley, as in Hemingway; no Sister Carrie, no Emma Bovary, no Candida, no Liza, no Major Barbara, no Molly Bloom, no Grushenka, no Rosalind; no Catherine Sloper, no Olive, no Verena, as in James.

Bellow undertook to order the meal for everyone, reading the menu with black horn-rimmed eyeglasses taken from his pocket. When the food came he said, "Here's the food, everybody salivate."

When I told him that I had been teaching *Dangling Man*—Book One, Step One, I said, on the long road of biography—he replied exactly as he had replied in October, "I haven't read that book in a long time." His thoughts seemed to dwell on it for a moment, bringing it back. I remarked upon its many foreshadowings of later work: for example, I said, the older brother, Amos, tries to force money on Joseph. I was beginning to see this, I said, as a pattern. Perhaps I would not have noticed it so soon but for my meeting with Irving Harris in October.

Bellow was surprised at this, saying he had never noticed a prevalence of brothers in his work. Now what was I to make of that? The novelist had not noticed his own pattern. Hard to believe. That part of me belonging to the Modern Language Association rebelled, resisted, resented the artist's denial of my scholarship. On the other hand, as a novelist, I could remember how often my eye had caught two passages written years apart, each time in the conviction that they were absolutely new, but seen finally as identical, repetitive, quite alike. Bellow has written of "the unknown process of the imagination. . . . Critics need to be reminded of this, I think."[5]

Stern told across the table of the new Troyat biography of Tolstoy, just published, which he was reading. He laughed with superior delight at Tolstoy's mindless oppression of his wife, from whom he demanded every service, and upon whom he blamed his woe. Easy to write a biography when your subject is dead! Anyone can do it.

At a nearby table sat Ernest Samuels, biographer of Henry Adams. I said to Bellow that I was of the opinion Henry Adams had written his own—who would be so redundant as to do again what was already imperishably done? I felt Bellow stir beside me, brace himself. Despicable critic, there I was, condemning years of work (three volumes, to be exact) of a man sitting five tables away. An author no sooner makes himself visible than a critic who has not read a line of his work descends upon him viciously with a mouth full of half-chewed Chinese food. Samuels tonight, Bellow tomorrow. Was that it? That might have been the stirring or the bracing I felt—the clear air slightly misting again.

For some reason, the meal felt hurried to me. We were something less than one big happy group: we were more a boardinghouse. We

5. "Distractions of a Fiction Writer," p. 6.

paid the bill individually, or by family, little as it was. Eighteen dollars for eleven people. How to divide eighteen by eleven? Stern became treasurer, the money was gathered, and Bellow introduced me to Ernest Samuels as we passed from the restaurant.

We had two cars. How to divide eleven by two? Bellow was carrying a painting in his car. I do not know what it was. He said it would not fit into his trunk. I felt that he was irritated—he would have preferred to drive alone, ten of us in the other car. Stern said that the painting *would* fit into Bellow's trunk. Stern and Bellow wore Cossack hats. Bellow reiterated that the painting would not fit. Stern urged Bellow to *try* to fit the painting into the trunk, and Bellow tried, and, indeed, it comfortably fit.

Now, how to distribute the people? Since Stern's car had a broken spring he felt that he should carry as few people as possible. Six went with Bellow, five with Stern. In Bellow's car everyone was hacking, coughing, and hoarsely rasping while trying to speak on one subject or another. When Gay Stern suggested that Bellow stop at a drugstore for medication for Miss Stat he somewhat illogically replied—or snarled, not at Gay but at Miss Stat—"I've got six people in this car, how can I stop at a drugstore?"

As for Miss Stat, I wonder where she thought all this would lead her. (Certainly not to a drug store.) I am sure it was a kind of fun for her to be the friend of an illustrious man, to learn valuable things from his company, to share his friends—a kind of accelerated education. Yet she might be cast off at any moment. Demmie, in *Humboldt's Gift*, "loved old brooches and rings . . . but what she mostly wanted of course was an engagement ring." One way to cast off such a young woman is to cause her to die "in a plane crash in South America"—exactly the fate of poor Demmie.

Perhaps Miss Stat accepted her early end to this career, a brief life, like the life of an athlete. Very likely she gave it little thought, and surely she was unaware of the full extent of her power. Did she read Bellow? If she had, she might have been able to distinguish more clearly between the captive and the keeper. Bellow's phenomenal short story, "A Father-to-be," is a fine concise account of his male helplessness against the flesh of women. In that story we see how "the life force . . . trampling on our individual humanity," imprisons Rogin, a bachelor, age thirty-one, all "on a snowy Sunday evening."

Rogin, a "research chemist," is on his way to supper with his fiancée at her apartment.

He rides the subway, his mind "strangely stimulated" by the motion of the train. Observing his fellow-passengers one after another, he soon begins intently to study "the man next to him. This was a man whom he had never in his life seen before but with whom he now suddenly felt linked through all existence."

And why not? For in Rogin's mind the man on the subway seat beside him becomes his son and Joan's. He has her skin, her blue eyes, her "straight and purely Roman nose . . . Forty years hence, a son of hers, provided she had one, might be like this. A son of hers? Of such a son, he himself, Rogin, would be the father. . . . Yes, think forty years ahead, and a man like this, who sat by him knee to knee in the hurtling car among their fellow-creatures, unconscious participants in a sort of great carnival of transit—such a man would carry forward what had been Rogin."

Rogin becomes increasingly depressed by the prospect of the future, he feels himself to be only an instrument, a creature of no will, cursed by this unpleasant son, this "fourth-rate man of the world." "The inhumanity of the next generation incensed Rogin. . . . What the blazes am I getting into?"

He arrives "tense" at Joan's apartment. She persuades him to allow her to wash his hair. His mind rehearses brave speeches proclaiming his equality, his right to be free of her, the injustice of his being her captive in spirit, even as he is her captive in flesh this very moment: "He sat with his breast against the cool enamel" while Joan "pressed against him from behind, surrounding him, pouring the water gently over him until it seemed to him that the water came from within him, it was the warm fluid of his own secret loving spirit overflowing into the sink, green and foaming, and the words he had rehearsed he forgot, and his anger at his son-to-be disappeared altogether, and he sighed, and said to her from the water-filled hollow of the sink, 'You always have such wonderful ideas, Joan. You know? You have a kind of instinct, a regular gift.'"

When we entered the Sterns' house Miss Stat lifted her feet, now the left foot, now the right foot, for Bellow to help her off with her big boots, stooping to do so. It struck me as anomalous that the oldest person present, a distinguished, silver-haired literary man revered across the world, should be down on haunches like a baseball catcher in the service of Miss Stat. Better the ill-tempered Bellow, who would not stop at the drugstore, than a servile Bellow propitiating! Nobody was in a better position to take off Miss Stat's boots than Miss Stat herself. I would not have taken off her boots or his. What had she to offer? A New York City taxicab driver complained to Herzog of the innocence of young women: "A broad eighteen don't even know how to shit."

I asked Stern if I might build a fire in the fireplace. Whether because of the fire, or for some other reason, our group became unified, as it had not been in the restaurant. We were ten, seated rather in a circle than a square, and I was pleased to see Bellow's spirits on the rise. At one point, then or soon, a moment occurred which was to be of some value to my own writing afterward: Stern and I were talking to each other of our work. His was going poorly, said Stern. Mine even worse, I said, I was bogged down in a novel, I couldn't go forward, I couldn't go backward, I couldn't abandon it, I was stumped, depressed. Bellow, overhearing this, urged me to try writing two works at once. Such a simple idea had never entered my mind, but I took it up with good results, have followed it ever since, and have urged it on many students who in turn have reported good results. Transaction completed in sixty seconds.

Soon the conversation had become extremely heated among Bellow, Blau, and Bluestone, over the question of the war in Vietnam. Miss Stat, after some hesitation, joined Blau and Bluestone—the whole of civilization was at stake, she said; something like that. In Bellow's view, this was true, but not in the way she meant it: opposition to the American role in Vietnam, he argued, was a denial of the memory of the failure of French pacifism in 1940. In some sense the dangling man was now no longer dangling. It was a change of heart or mind I would understand better after I had read "The Old System," scale model for *Mr. Sammler's Planet*. Dr. Braun and Mr. Sammler were the figures Bellow was trying out now. They were who he was becoming, or who he was becoming closer *to*, as the full horror of man's capacity for wickedness became more real to him.

He was speaking as well out of an extreme skepticism of the youth movement in the United States in 1967. Every youth movement, Bellow contended, led to tyranny. An ideological American Left was impossible—its young smart leaders are soon called to Washington for $15,000 a year to supply the government with ideas. Ferment led only to ferment: we could not afford to establish a precedent of the rule of youth. "The children were setting fire to the libraries," Mr. Sammler reflects, rolling through Manhattan in his nephew's chauffeur-driven Rolls Royce. "And putting on Persian trousers, letting their sideburns grow. This was their symbolic wholeness. An oligarchy of technicians, engineers, the men who run the grand machines, infinitely more sophisticated than this automobile, would come to govern vast slums filled with bohemian adolescents, narcotized, beflowered, and 'whole.' He himself was a fragment, Mr. Sammler understood."

Miss Stat received Bellow's criticism of young people rather personally. She became agitated, coughing a great deal. Whenever we laughed we were required to pause until the general hacking, the coughing, and the bronchial croaking subsided. Once Bellow dealt with Miss Stat with sarcasm—fed up with her and with all of us. Someone had mentioned Gilbert Seldes. Miss Stat asked who he was. Bellow replied, "The father of Timothy Seldes."

Some of us agreed that the convention of the MLA had left us melancholy, a mood from which Bellow lifted us with tales of his difficult academic past. His humor, touched with bitterness, led to a moment difficult in the extreme. Like many successful persons, Bellow carried the wounds of early struggle. Insults galore. Retroactive recognition. Bellow has told in writing of his meeting in 1952 with a former Chicago associate well-connected in New York, who was surprised and basically offended to hear of Bellow's having won a small job at Princeton. "It had never occurred to him that I might be connected with anything so classy, and because of his respect for higher learning, probably absorbed from [Chancellor Hutchins], he was upset. So I was very sorry, and I said, 'It's only temporary.' 'What do your academic colleagues think about that?' he said. 'Oh, it's probably a joke to them, but they still have most of the joint to themselves. What's the matter, Mack? Why does this bother you?' 'Well,' he said, 'writers have always come out of the gutter. The gutter is their proper place.' I can't think just now which of the one hundred Great Books of the Western World contains this historic idea."[6]

Academically, Bellow for some time was "connected with nothing." His tenure was the gutter. His scholarly efforts had turned to stories, he had never earned a doctoral degree, and before he had

6. "The University as Villain," *The Nation*, November 16, 1957, pp. 361–62.

won prizes or earned money even well-intentioned academics had a hard time knowing whether his work was good. On several occasions, I take it, Bellow was hurt, demeaned, put down, badly seen by people who, once scorning him as a gutter type, would afterward claim him. These old memories would become the spice of *Humboldt's Gift*.

At this moment, before Stern's fireside, Bellow indulged a certain coolness toward Lionel Trilling. Trilling was "a reformed rabbi," a worldly rabbi, a type for whom Bellow expresses considerable contempt—the "Madison Avenue" rabbi "with his . . . public-relations air, did not go for these European Judaic, operatic fist-clenchings. Tears. He made the cantor tone it down."[7] Fifth Avenue synagogues (synagogos?): "Mr. Sammler, thinking of Rabbi Ipsheimer, whom he had been dragged by Shula to hear, revised the old saying. Artificial pearls before real swine were cast by these jet-set preachers." A rabbi ought to be ascetic, of the old system, the old poverty. It was the Americanization of the rabbi which offended Bellow, the Americanization of the Jewish spirit, the dilution of the devotion: Isaac Braun, erecting "ugly" buildings, kept the Psalms in the glove compartment of his Cadillac. Lake Shore Jews?

Modern, contemptible rabbis smoke cigarettes and chase women. Trilling retained the cigarette but lost the calling. He became a worldly academic. Bellow told of an occasion when he, Trilling, and Harry Levin had served on a committee to award a literary prize. Bellow wished to award the prize to Flannery O'Connor, but he was outvoted by Trilling and Levin, who favored John O'Hara.

I could hardly believe it. Bellow could hardly believe it, either. Nobody in the room could believe it. According to Bellow, Trilling said that O'Hara was the only writer he could read "while indisposed." For that reason Trilling awarded O'Hara the prize. The prize committee adjourned. Bellow encountered Trilling in the men's room, where Trilling "by mistake," said Bellow, "was pissing in his shoes." Bellow tried to decide for himself how to be most helpful, the "Talmudic" thing to do: whether, on one hand, to tell Trilling he was pissing in his shoes; or, on the other, to ignore it. "By the time I made up my mind," said Bellow, "he was done."

7. "The Old System," *Playboy*, January 1968, p. 245.

As for someone else we all knew, he was "a Harvard kike."

I was shocked to hear Bellow employ such an expression. My attention was suddenly diverted from one injustice to another: my head was yanked rudely from one side to the other. A small comedy suddenly became serious, full of disturbing implications. My enthusiasm for Bellow plummeted. As Josephine unhappily perceived the figure of the fictional Herzog in the living Bellow, so I now heard this private exclamation I'd need somehow to come to terms with. Maybe I should report Bellow to Mr. Abt of the Anti-Defamation League—that fellow with whom we had stood among the burning leaves. *Take back America's Legacy Award, your silver medallion,* I'd say. How terrible to think of Bellow sunk to the level of my Minneapolis barbershop friend—"Nothing very vicious. Only a touch of the old stuff"—but not very interesting, either. Updike in *Bech* had referred to Bech's "quixotic, excessively tender, strangely anti-Semitic Semitic sensibility."[8] Updike cute again, I had thought, everything shrouded in fancy words. But now?

Well, an eccentricity, an idiosyncrasy, a quirk. If there were Lake Shore Jews there were Harvard kikes. (In *Humboldt's Gift* "candy store kikes." "These social wars are nothing to me," says Charlie Citrine. "And let's not forget all the hard things you've said about Ivy League kikes." Roger Kahn has told in a magazine article of a Las Vegas car dealer named Kelly the Kike. But even in Las Vegas such bad taste was outlawed. And now I am told by a reader of this manuscript that one of the golden moments of the Watergate tapes was Nixon's reference to his ardent defender, Rabbi Baruch Korff, as "a kike rabbi.")

I felt his bad word keenly. I did not really for the moment wish to go on with him. My friend Bluestone, linguist, democratic zealot, for whom the word was the signal of deepest meaning, was unforgiving. With him, I wanted things said right by the right process. At lunch the next day Bluestone and I talked of nothing else. Bluestone was offended not because he was Harvard and Jewish, but in principle. He would have objected equally to Harvard wop . . . nigger . . . mick . . . and if the moment had occurred not in the Sterns' house but at the convention of the Modern Language Association he

8. (New York: Alfred A. Knopf, 1970), p. 71.

would have made an issue of it, calling for an apology, a retraction, demanding here or there a resignation, producing a petition, penetrating whatever affliction the suspicious word might signify.

Three cheers for the MLA! Its passion was decorum, process, gentility, responsibility, documentation, control, and a true conservation. People there were careful with their tongues, nor were they difficult, as Bellow was—there hadn't been a woodchuck in the Palmer House. If I had an appointment with someone he or she was there. If I telephoned someone he answered. If I wrote him a letter he received it, even if I wrote it in France.

My friend Blau, on the other hand, forgave; or took it lightly. He saw Bellow's carelessness as gesture, impulse, the private flight of an artist. Years as a director of theater had taught Blau to accept the craziness of performers as inextricable from the ultimate performance. "Derangement" was a word common with Blau, and he tolerated a great deal of it among actors, writers, musicians, designers, and other artists who would never be complete or thorough thinkers. Bellow, said Blau, must be thought of as "temperamentally exempt." He required his compulsions and obsessions if he were to discover the work ahead. To condemn Bellow's private speech was as foolish as condemning unrevised, provisional, exploratory writing-in-progress, fishing in the wastebasket.

It was my duty, said Blau, to understand that biographers cannot be choosers. If I was on the whole devoted to my subject I must not fall into disillusionment at the first disappointment. It went with the territory. Only the newborn babe was pure—and Blau wasn't even sure about him. Very well, *temperamentally exempt*, I would try to take it in, receive it, absorb it.

Ill, coughing, hacking, someone telephoned for two taxicabs. We were told that they were unavailable. Bellow somewhat grudgingly agreed to drive one contingent (Bluestone and the Fussells) to the Palmer House, but he was preserved from that when a taxicab coincidentally appeared. Thus Stern drove the Palmer House contingent, and the Blaus and Harrises made their way by coincidental cab to the Knickerbocker.

I was heavy-hearted about Bellow's biography. Bellow's views on Vietnam discouraged me. And "Harvard kike" cast me down altogether. Men had broken over less. In *Henderson the Rain King*

Charlie, newly married, breaks abruptly with Henderson—"all be-cause," Henderson explains, "I had forgotten to kiss his wife after the ceremony. . . . I attended the wedding and stood up for him. However, because I forgot to kiss the bride after the ceremony, there developed a coolness on her side and eventually she became my enemy."

Chapter Six

LISTLESSLY, back at Purdue, I wrote up my journal of our December visit, from the hour of our driving to Chicago to the moment of our departing the Sterns' house in a taxicab. I now had seventy pages of detailed memoranda expanded by typewriter from notes taken by hand. In ten years I would have seven hundred pages from which to form a book—straight through the two presidential terms of Richard Nixon and halfway through the first term of Spiro Agnew—unless, of course, my fading interest faded totally. My wife was not too crazy about him. My friend Bluestone was upset. Blau granted him his temperament. Bellow seemed to disapprove my daughter. I had friends in San Francisco who weren't too fond of Bellow, and by the end of the year that number of San Franciscans would rapidly increase, as we shall see.

But the new year had hardly begun when Bellow's story, "The Old System," appeared in *Playboy*, whereupon everything he may have lacked of charm or discretion seemed not to matter. The work transcended the creator. In "The Old System" Dr. Braun's memory frames a family history enwrapped in a story—childhood, first fleshly passion, madness, marriage, moneymaking, swindling, affluence, fortune, failure, and death. A nice Jewish family. Within the story, Dr. Braun is the ethical center. In him is the gene of memory. He is witness, interpreter, content to be powerless and peaceful, demanding not Heaven but only earth, *this* planet which is, as Mr. Sammler will express it, "our mother and our burial ground."

Although I was still somewhat negative about Bellow I could not help but write him a letter praising "The Old System"—"I just thought I'd say what a beautiful and wonderful story I think *The Old System* is. . . . It succeeds in the best way, that's all, rich in time, rich in detail, and so *moving* at the end, which may be what things should do, but so seldom do, *move* me." My revival of interest in Bellow seems also to have been accompanied by a relapse into the self-consciousness of my earlier presentation of myself; into a show of independence from him, for in the same letter I wrote: "I really do wish I knew my plans for the next academic year. . . . Why not go back to San Francisco and live by the stock market? Is that somehow ignoble?" I'd have never made it in the stock market. I had neither the temperament nor the money. I didn't even have $60,000.

He replied with a pleasant postcard: "It was kind of you to write about the story. I was pleased, touched, delighted. That kind of thing is what I mean to write. Always meant to write. Always thought that this was what writing was about. A few people responded to it as you did. Most, I suppose, don't know what to make of it. Afraid it may not be the *thing*? Afraid of being Square? Worried that Susan Sontag might not like it? To this we seem to have come. I enjoyed our evening with Blau and Stern. I liked meeting your wife, whom I instantly admired. Ever yrs, Saul."

Showing him how rich I was, I'd show him too how balanced I was. He should think of his biographer as responsible, staid, steady, sane, reliable. I had written in that spirit an article for the *Atlantic* on the "hippies" of San Francisco, and sent it to Bellow through Stern. Bellow said he never received it, although Stern assured me he had passed it along. I sent another in the mail, but Bellow said he never received the second copy, either.

In April I sent him a copy of a paper I had written dealing in part with *Dangling Man*. He did not acknowledge my paper, although I thought it was excellent. In my teaching I had gone from *Dangling Man* to *The Victim*—"taking you up that way two books a year," I wrote to him, but that did not especially interest him. I read Bellow while teaching him, as he perhaps read Wells, Tawney, Laski, Strachey, Orwell, in preparation for the character of Mr. Sammler. "Continuing my campaign to take up one Bellow each semester," I wrote to him some months later, "I'll be teaching *Henderson* in a course in 'black literature,' especially included in the curriculum so that Purdue might meet the demands of Negro students." Suiting my idea of his outlook on such subjects as special courses for Negro students, I added: "I am going to fool the students: coming for sociology, they're going to get literature. I hope they don't lynch me."

I had written to him in the spring that "I was sort of hoping to go to Chicago one of these days," but that trip never came about. I failed to rouse myself. Nor did he encourage me. He was silent. By summer I had abandoned all Chicago plans, flimsy to begin with. I invited him to be my guest in San Francisco in the summer, giving him all my digits—Box 14037, zip 94114, telephone 415-431-9949—but, unknown to me, he had gone there, instead, in May.

On Friday, May 10, 1968, in West Lafayette, Indiana, I wrote forward in my novel, *The Goy*, took lunch with four colleagues, visited a dying man, read Faulkner for class, and declined to sign an advertisement supporting Robert Kennedy for president, on the grounds that I had already signed one supporting Eugene McCarthy. Within a month Kennedy was assassinated in Los Angeles. A month earlier Martin Luther King had been assassinated in Memphis. Somebody was dying because somebody was nervous. Increasingly difficult to feel that the American system was the best of all systems! In a war we could not stop, our young men were shipped abroad and quickly killed. At home our most promising leaders were gunned to death, perhaps by the same people who advocated perpetual war abroad. Orwell writes this: "It is the same in all wars; the soldiers do the fighting, the journalists do the shouting, and no true patriot ever gets near a front-line trench, except on the briefest of propaganda tours. Sometimes it is a comfort to me to think that the aeroplane is altering the conditions of war. Perhaps when the next great war comes we may see that sight unprecedented in all history, a jingo with a bullet-hole in him."[1] I was becoming a leader of the antiwar movement at Purdue, thinking that by discussion, education, and teaching we might help to build a society without guns; seeing it begin to happen; thinking we might go all the way to Utopia; anyhow, hoping so, with Bellow.

1. George Orwell, *Homage to Catalonia* (New York: Harcourt, Brace and World, 1969), p. 66.

Bellow, on that Friday, was speaking at San Francisco State College; my former employer: I had taught there for thirteen years. According to the city newspaper "an overflowing audience of at least 700 students" was there—wrong as usual, for not everyone there was a student. One at least was Hannah Koler, godmother to my son Henry, whom Bellow would have recognized as a version of Dr. Braun or Mr. Sammler, the ethical, artistic survivor of a spreading family, recently European, hustlers, makers, doers, aggressive first sons grown rich purveying junk. She loved good things with a critical eye, supporting them with her means as she was able, art, books, music. I first heard the word "ecology" from her. At age seventy or thereabouts she walked the San Francisco streets in the first of the peace marches; a political liberal, yes, but more than that; her politics was the politics of humor, of psychological insight, of the perception of fakes and moral idiots and antihumanists by minimal clues. She was an agent of formal culture. The most likely place to meet her by chance was in the lobby of a concert hall, at a lecture. At peace with herself, she was therefore capable of imagining peace in the world; a breathless, smiling woman, slightly stouter as she aged, urging peace as the loveliest way, after all, to comfort and joy in a short life.

In every way an amateur, she was an amateur writer, too. Her report of Bellow's speaking engagement, contained in a letter to Josephine, surpasses in interest and relevance the professional report of the newspaper.

> Dearest Jo . . . There's so much going on at State College these days. I s'pose it has reached your papers—I will send you some clippings separately from the Chronicle. Today's paper says, the tumult has subsided—
>
> The day, David and Harriet arrived (about 11 AM May 10) we went direct from the airport to State to hear Saul Bellows—He was an exciting speaker—witty, entertaining & definitely cynical—A packed to the doors audience—all went well until the question period—when one young fellow who had come in for the last 5 minutes began with a needling question—like 'Why didn't you name Herzog—Bellows?' Bellows answered very sharply something to the tone of 'mind your own business'—the next moment the questioner went beserk & used the most

obscene language maligning his character & even accusing him of sex inadequacy. It left a terrible sour note on an otherwise stimulating talk. Somehow I felt, Bellows invited this by reacting very sharply to questioners—he lacked graciousness, courtesy or an attitude of sympathetic understanding. This opinion I will expand on when we are together. The student in question was a Phillipino I believe—it broke up the meeting at once—

As you know, student rebellion is taking place all over—Columbia U. in N.Y. & the universities in France now, etc.—the universities are where the future leaders of the world will come from—and they are in rebellion now—I hope they will have a more peaceful unchaotic world to lead when their turn comes. . . . Happy Journey Home!

"Then Feffer led him into a large room." So begins that passage of *Mr. Sammler's Planet* telling of the hero's dismaying experience at Columbia University.

He had expected a small one, a seminar room. He had come to reminisce, for a handful of interested students . . . But this was a mass meeting of some sort. . . . The amphitheater was filled. Standing room only. Was Feffer running one of his rackets? . . . A microphone was hung on his chest. . . . "I assume," he said, "you are acquainted with the background, the events of nineteen seventeen. You know of the mutinous armies, the February Revolution in Russia, the disasters that befell authority . . ."

Doubly foreign, Polish-Oxonian, with his outrushing white back hair, the wrinkles streaming below the smoked glasses, he pulled the handkerchief from his breast pocket, unfolded and refolded it, touched his face, wiped his palms with thin elderly delicacy. Without pleasure in performance, without the encouragement of attention (there was a good deal of noise), the little satisfaction he did feel was the meager ghost of the pride he and his wife had once taken in their British successes. . . . Sammler, with growing interest and confidence recalling all this, lectured on *Cosmopolis* for half an hour, feeling what a kindhearted, ingenuous, stupid scheme it had been. Telling this into the lighted restless hole of the amphitheater with the soiled dome and caged electric fixtures, until he was interrupted by a clear loud voice. He was being questioned. He was being shouted at.

"Hey!"

He tried to continue. "Such attempts to draw intellectuals away from Marxism met with small success. . . ."

A man in Levi's, thick-bearded but possibly young, a figure of compact distortion, was standing shouting at him.

"Hey! Old Man!"

In the silence, Mr. Sammler drew down his tinted spectacles, seeing this person with his effective eye.

"Old Man! You quoted Orwell before."

"Yes?"

"You quoted him to say that British radicals were all protected by the Royal Navy? Did Orwell say that British radicals were protected by the Royal Navy?"

"Yes, I believe he did say that."

"That's a lot of shit."

Sammler could not speak.

"Orwell was a fink. He was a sick counterrevolutionary. It's good he died when he did. And what you are saying is shit." Turning to the audience, extending violent arms and raising his palms like a Greek dancer, he said, "Why do you listen to this effete old shit? What has he got to tell you? His balls are dry. He's dead. He can't come."

Sammler later thought that voices had been raised on his side. Someone had said, "Shame. Exhibitionist."

But no one really tried to defend him. Most of the young people seemed to be against him. The shouting sounded hostile. Feffer was gone, had been called away to the telephone. Sammler, turning from the lectern, found his umbrella, trench coat, and hat behind him and left the platform, guided by a young girl who had rushed up to express indignation and sympathy, saying it was a scandal to break up such a good lecture. She showed him through a door, down several stairs, and he was on Broadway at One hundred-sixteenth Street.

Abruptly out of the university.

Back in the city.

At Purdue University, neither coastal nor urban, everything happened merely slightly later. I ate my lunch out of a brown bag in the windowless commons room on the fourth (windowless) floor of Heavilon Hall. Professor Bob Miller had hung in his office a photograph showing what you'd see if he had a window, but the world blew in through the air-conditioning, and professors talked of books, writers, writing, and the world of print and printing gleaned from magazines, reviews, quarterlies, international newspapers, publishers' announcements, and people in other Departments of English everywhere. They were earnest, hostile, humorous, bitter, envious, sometimes surprisingly intuitive, sometimes touchingly respectful, innocent enough to be careless of the lives of the writers they devoured for lunch, and I often sullenly thought, "I don't dare leave this room for fear of what they'll say."

As the war in Vietnam continued we talked in the commons room less about literature. Local skirmishes and scrimmages increased. One of the antiwar Chicago Seven spoke unprecedented dirty words from the stage of the Elliott Hall of Music, students marched, paraded, wore obscene pins and slogans, strafed the Union, insulted alumni, and took as one of their campus heroes the writer William Gass. To Gass's work, apart from his leadership against the war, I was not especially attracted, but I cheered him for his rallying students and faculty alike.

The English Department preferred Bellow to Gass by a wide margin, and my acquaintance with Bellow was a definite point in my favor. My good friend and office-mate, Chester Eisinger, had written devotedly of Bellow, and my good friend (later antagonist) of the commons room, Mark Rowan, admired Bellow's work in a manner sincere, loving, and complete.

We had also in our department a young man named Lycette, who was for a time determined to work on Bellow until Eisinger stopped him. Lycette had no aptitude for Bellow, but he believed he could write a swift dissertation upon the subject, and I am sure he could.

He eventually wrote also a pamphlet on *Herzog* for Cliff's Notes, a series of dilutions prepared for students too much in a hurry to read a whole book. The swift shall lead the hurried. Lycette's pamphlet contains no word of Bellow's own. Complicated characters are reduced to a few lines in a section called "Character Analyses," following a section which had reduced the novel to nine parts, each part sprinkled all over with symbols. For example, Herzog riding on a train "symbolizes the hero's internal journey toward self-understanding," while a fish market, "overcast sky, the polluted river nearby, the brackish air, and the fish packed together in ice—all these are symbols of Herzog's fragmented life." The pamphlet concludes with "Review Questions" and "Theme Topics" for teachers and students too regularly on the run to ask any questions of themselves. I especially adore "10. What are the purposes of Herzog's memories of the dead, especially of his family? . . . 14. Is the protagonist mad or sane? Defend your conclusion."

If there were no purpose to remembering the dead, Lycette would dismiss them from his mind. No waste motion. Speed, speed. Remembering the dead, I remember Mark Rowan in the commons room, he and his tobacco, and I. We had been boys together, not in place but in spirit, sharing the lore of the Thirties in sports, radio, politics, savoring the words of heroes worshipped in common. Our heads echoed the same tunes, and we were prone to the same puns.

Questions of public decorum finally came between us. Obscenity from the stage of Elliott Hall of Music hurt him deeply in ways the killing in Vietnam did not. Obscenity may be for books, but not for the daily press; one may swear at will in the commons room of the English Department, but not in Elliott Hall. The issue of the war became centered for us upon the issue of dirty words, and we went at it, we fought, we screamed at one another, the commons room was abandoned by our colleagues to our exclusive dispute between sandwich halves, and I went off to class distressed and undigested. In fact, we were fond of one another in the extreme. Sometimes I could have killed him. His tobacco finally did.

Above all, we shared Bellow, which Mark Rowan knew in detail. Mark Rowan knew Joseph, Asa, Augie, all the rest, and when he knew that I also knew Bellow the person he congratulated me upon my extreme good fortune. Upon that issue we agreed, surely.

Therefore, said Mark Rowan, we must invite Bellow to Purdue to give a talk.

Bless them, professors of English, for all their inside dope on the private lives of writers, for all their commons-room confidence of methods, intentions, purposes, lose much of their certainty over questions of fact. Would Bellow come if we asked him? What was his probable fee? These things we could learn by asking, which introduced the kind of question invulnerable to sheerest speculation: where did he receive his mail?

Logical that I should be empowered to invite Bellow to speak to us! I was delighted. Without delay, I wrote to him with "a small proposition to offer you: the man in charge of an English Department lecture series asks me to ask you whether you would come here under the following circumstances: to give one talk to a group which will probably be mainly people interested in literature, and to visit informally with students, probably mainly graduate students. That would be on an afternoon of your choosing any time from February 1 to May, for a fee of $250 plus traveling expenses."

Three months earlier I had written to Bellow in praise of "Mosby's Memoirs," which had appeared in *The New Yorker*. He had replied appreciatively, adding voluntarily his colorful version of the event at San Francisco: "The thing at S.F. State was very bad. I'm not too easy to offend at my age [53], and I don't think I was personally affronted—that's not my style. The thing was offensive though. Being denounced by Salas as an old shit to an assembly which seemed to find the whole thing deliciously thrilling. Being told furthermore that 'this is an effete old man—he can't *come!*' My impulse was to say, 'Let's choose a young lady from the audience for a trial heat and see about this.' But the young lady wouldn't have known the difference between one man and another. One glance at the audience told me this. So I left the platform in defeat. Undefended by the bullied elders of the faculty. While your suck-up-to-the-young colleagues swallowed their joyful saliva. No, it was very poor stuff, I assure you. You don't found universities in order to destroy culture. For that you want a Nazi party. Enough said. Thanks again and all best . . ."

With that account in mind, I added to my invitation: "I myself hope that you will do this, for it will give me an opportunity to get more of you into my Journal and record, though I suppose that might not be much inducement to *you*. On the other hand, I can guarantee you that the experience here will not be like the horror you describe at San Francisco State; these things don't shift from place to place just because I do."

But of course things do shift from place to place, smuggled in hearts and brains past all border guards. Therefore I could "guarantee" no such thing as safety from the kind of experience Bellow had

had in San Francisco. Nor could I even guarantee Bellow or anyone that I truly thought "the horror" all that horrible. I had no idea how I might have behaved had I been in San Francisco at that hour. Perhaps I would have avoided the auditorium. But how could I have not attended Bellow speaking? To go or not to go. Or if I went, and it happened as it happened, would I have responsibly leaped to my feet and called for order, respect? Or would I have burst into flame like Salas the "Phillipino" (Mexican, actually), linking Bellow to that slaughter of children called war, demanding of Bellow that he take his stand against the war in the clearest immediate current phrases —never mind history, never mind culture, never mind a Nazi party. Love and literature were nothing to the issue: Boswell stoned his father's house for politics.

I was delighted not to have been there. But I *was* at Purdue now, and if Bellow came I might discover myself allied not with literature or with the long past ("These things cast outward by a great begetting spasm billions of years ago," Dr. Braun thinks, looking at the stars at day's end) but with the crisis of the immediate. Indeed, anticipating Bellow's visit, I might get on the telephone with Bill Gass. He'd stir the natives up. "Bill, dust off the bullhorn, there's a war on. The Yiddish are coming. Question his sex adequacy."

For the moment, the question remained moot. Bellow did not reply. Perhaps the fee was too little for the time, the labor. Perhaps he did not care to talk into my journal. Perhaps he never received my letter.

NOVEMBER PASSED to March. I did not communicate with Bellow. I completed my novel. "I have just yesterday sent off my new novel and am feeling very good about it," I wrote to Stern. "But I feel horrible living here and not seeing you and Saul. . . . I wish there were an opportunity to go up to Chicago and view you." (When Bellow heard of my novel entitled *The Goy* he wrote: "Let me say, though, that to publish a novel under such a title as *The Goy* is in my opinion a sad mistake. I hope you will think twice about it or even more than twice. As you know I do no propaganda for any ethnic groups whatever. The only consideration is one of taste. With this caveat I am . . ." I had never thought of "goy" as a hate-word. "Kike" yes.)

On April 30 I wrote to Stern again: ". . . a whole year or more has gone by, simply wasted as far as my biography of S. Bellow is concerned. It's a shame not to be seeing him and taking notes, eavesdropping on his life. Just for my own sake, if not for literary glory, it would be well for me to see him. I learn much from him."

Summer came. Back to San Francisco. Summer went. Back to Indiana.

October. Flying from Indiana to Oregon, changing planes in Chicago, I telephoned Stern. Then Bellow. Stern was preparing for his day's classes—it was morning, a Wednesday—and yet we talked for half an hour. His enthusiasm wound him up.

Bellow was even this moment, Stern said, reading galleys of his new novel. For the *Atlantic*. I suffered a twinge there. Mike Janeway, editor of the *Atlantic*, had just turned down *my* new novel. Yet I was a close friend of his mother. He was rejecting his mother.

"You think his new book is really good," I said.

"He's *exploded* with it," said Stern.

"The one with *Moon* in the title?" I asked.

"Changed now to *Planet*," said Stern. "You know, Saul *believes* in fiction," said Stern. Bellow was unlike certain other writers, said Stern, for whom "real events leave no place for the imagination." This was well said. Why, after all, had I been reading Bellow again from start to finish, knowing a need for his fiction, feeling no need at all for reports of "real" events of the sort reported by the media? Only fine writing told me the things I needed to know, told me everything, embraced events, going in and out of varieties of consciousness. Bellow's research was his intuition, revelation, wide-ranging guessing.

"Two years in the midwest now," I lamented to Stern—starting my third year: by now I should have gathered bushels of notes and biographical material pertaining to Bellow. And this would be my last year here. Back to California.

"Saul thinks," said Stern, "that I should have something ready to print about him in case he goes down in an airplane."

I was about to board an airplane. "Not that he feared flying, but . . ." Herzog remembers a crash "over Maryland recently, when human figures were seen to spill and fall like shelled peas." Soon I would read *Herzog* again, fragments of which I had first heard from Bellow in the house at Tivoli. Wearing a hat while he read. Semester by semester I had come back through his books. On then to *Mr. Sammler's Planet*, the newest work of my still-groping biographee, my unfinished subject, my active friend not yet *fini*. Maybe I should try a biography of somebody dead. I mentioned that to Stern. Or if not dead, said Stern, a one-book man or woman, or a young writer who had written one or two great things in a very short life and immediately died, or a child prodigy short-story writer dead at age six.

Bellow on the telephone. Irritable, too. Cranky. Of course, he was reading galleys, eager to get them done. But why the *Atlantic*? Why not *Playboy* for $10,000? That figure had stuck in my mind, unless Bellow had been boasting of fees, counter-boasting my $60,000 socked away in mutual funds. I didn't ask. I said only that I was eager to see him. Going on two years now since I had seen him. Well, he said, he was buried in these galleys, he had just been to New York "to rescue things," but he wasn't sure he had rescued anything—he was dissatisfied with these *Atlantic* galleys.

"Why New York?" I asked. "I thought *Atlantic* was in Boston."

"I went to New *York*," he said. "This isn't the occasion for geographical discussion"—he was pressed, he thought he'd say good-bye: "Good-bye, Mark." That moment depressed me, then and now. He was firm with me. But then he said, upon some relenting second-thought or other, "How is Lafayette?"

"As well as can be expected," I replied.

"Because you're a nice Jewish boy like me you make the best of everything," he said. Between the moment of his saying good-bye and his resumption of conversation—for it was now a brand-new conversation—some "sympathetic impression" had recalled itself to his mind; perhaps some memory of my being one of the few remaining writers who gave him "the time of day anymore." He collected himself, recalling that I was not some bloodsucking critic but someone who had read every word of him not once, not only twice, someone "teaching" him now. Then, too, a nice Jewish boy like him, one more check on his memory, one more adjustment of the mechanism bringing me into focus. People *did* keep forgetting I was a Jew. And then when once they had that fully absorbed they met Josephine, and it all got lost again because nobody took her for a Jew. My friend Herbert Blau for years and years went on making jokes about our "mixed marriage." No matter how many times we reminded him, he instantly forgot. "Because you're a nice Jewish boy like me," said Bellow, fixing it in mind, "you make the best of everything."

"I suppose so," I said. "Nevertheless we're going back to California next year and work for Blau."

"So you're leaving the middle west," said Bellow, bravely accepting. "We must have a party for you."

"I don't want a party," I said. "I don't like arrangements."

"We'll just go to dinner then," he said. He asked me a few details of Blau's school, the California Institute of the Arts. He mentioned Robert Corrigan, who would be its president. Yet I had called it "Blau's school," and his ear caught that. Bellow had strong feelings about both men, he knew the difference, and the difference identified me, too. He said, "You'll find good things in the new book."

"Jesus," I said, "*good things!* A new book of yours is going to be more than *good things.*" *Mr. Sammler's Planet* was a long leap beyond *Herzog*, and Bellow surely knew that. Yet, with a long leap of growth he already foresaw popular loss. Thus, not *Playboy* but *Atlantic.* Less money. A fainter name to younger readers. Worst of all, the satisfaction of the vultures. "Lots of people are waiting for me to fall on my face," says Humboldt, the man of experience, to the novice Charlie Citrine. "I have a million enemies." He likens the literary world to "the Cannibal Society of the Kwakiutl Indians"—if "the candidate . . . makes a ritual mistake the whole crowd tears him to pieces."

Even so, it was necessary to face those galleys, and necessary to bring out the book. I began to understand why he so often fled to far places: in America, bringing out a book is a miserable experience, worse than a crime, judging by the frenzy of reviewers. (A playwright once said, after reading bad reviews of his opening night: "The axe murderer on page one was treated better.") No wonder Bellow rushed off to Spain, Turkey, Yugoslavia, Rome, cheap countries recommended by Julius Citrine, the Dolomites, and Block Island by rowboat. Stern has written: "Our lunch may be lethal, our air unbreathable, our houses flimsy lumps, but there they are. As for the twenty or thirty novelists who mean something to us, we look them over closely."[2] Flowers. Mere flowers. "Once more the boom is lowered on the flowers."

I mentioned my own forthcoming book. I'd send him a copy. He complained of the title. He asked for publishing details. But when I began to tell him he began to retreat from the telephone, thoughts of

2. *The Books in Fred Hampton's Apartment* (London: Hamish Hamilton, 1974), p. 25.

the ordeal of his own galleys pressing in upon him. "Good-bye, Mark," he said, and then again more firmly, in a chilly manner, a second turn of mood, that old tricky double reverse, back to the farewell with which he had begun, prior to our conversation, coming forward thereafter through greetings, this time not to return. "Good-*bye*, Mark," he said, "Good-*bye*, Mark."

Chapter Seven

THERE WAS at Purdue University at that time a young man, assistant professor of English, who was pale and smooth of cheek (he had virtually no beard at all) and as earnest and conscientious and devoted and innocent and nervous and untenured as any young man in that situation, with whom I argued in the commons room on several occasions the truly relevant question whether professional football players were happy.

I cared nothing for the question. It was a way of arguing something else. That is to say, it was a way of conveying to Joel Burke if I could (for that was the name of the beardless man) the idea almost at the heart of literature, that things may not be what they appear to be, that certain persons of the world (for example, professional football players) who may appear to other persons to be living lives of singular ease, affluence, and security may indeed be less fortunate even than a pale, untenured assistant professor of English. A football player may on the whole be poorly paid and poorly used, exploited, his body broken and ruined, although it was undeniably true that one or two players in a hundred escaped ordinary fate, rising to be "stars," even "super-stars," worthy of Joel Burke's envy.

But no. No life for Joel Burke could be worse than his own. So it appeared to him. So it may have been. He could believe nothing except that his was a rare case—that he was one of the most unhappy men for miles around; that everyone else was beautifully secure; that he was poor and all men were rich.

I never heard him remark upon the blissful life of soldiers in Vietnam. He must have seen something of that on television, where he saw heroes of football. Television's supreme achievement was Instant Replay, and Joel Burke followed the games with care, rooting for the athletes he favored, dreaming of their wealth, seldom observing their melting away unnoticed, unmentioned. Would that he had studied war by Instant Replay.

Novelists, too, Burke knew, were monolithic, a closed corporation, all novelists knowing and loving all other novelists, gathering together frequently to count their money.

This being true, I should have no difficulty, Burke informed me, in persuading Saul Bellow to be Guest Speaker at the annual Literary Awards Banquet. Burke was chairman of the arrangements committee.

But this matter, I replied, had come up a year ago, I had written to Bellow offering him two hundred and fifty dollars, and he had ignored my letter; he ignored "torrents" of mail, I heard.

"But you can persuade him," said Burke.

"The last time I talked to him on the telephone," I said (one month ago; it was November now), "he kept emphasizing one idea only: the idea of good-bye."

"We'll pay him a thousand dollars," said Professor Burke.

"That might induce him," I said.

"I know it's only a token fee," said Burke.

"It's not a token," I said. "It's real money, a thousand."

"I know it's nothing to him," said Burke.

"What's nothing to him?"

"A thousand dollars."

"Really?"

Really. Right. I had Joel Burke's word for it. It was not the thousand token dollars Bellow might possibly come to Purdue for, but for me, only for me. Novelists stuck together. I alone could persuade Bellow to come to Purdue. That was Burke's conviction.

Burke supplied me not only with this new faith in myself but with two additional arguments with which to persuade Bellow of the beauty of the opportunity. First, I should tell Bellow the names of all the distinguished writers who had in the past appeared at the Literary Awards Banquet. He gave me a copy of a partial list. In the margin of the page appear in my own handwriting the words "empirically derived." Later, in the program for the banquet, the complete list was presented.

1928	Zona Gale	1950	John Crowe Ransom
1929	Elmer Davis	1951	Warren Beck
1930	Carl Sandburg	1952	William Carlos
1931	Sherwood Anderson		Williams
1932	James Weber Linn	1953	Louis Kronenberger
1933	Thornton Wilder	1954	Malcolm Cowley
1934	Christopher Morley	1955	J. Frank Dobie
1935	Stephen Leacock	1956	Randall Jarrell
1936	Theodore Dreiser	1957	Lillian Hellman
1937	William Allen White	1958	John Ciardi
1938	Thomas Wolfe	1959	John Crowe Ransom
1939	Carl Van Doren	1960	Richard Eberhart
1940	Robert Frost	1961	Herbert Gold
1941	Mary Ellen Chase	1962	William Golding
1942	President Edward	1963	Howard Nemerov
	C. Elliott	1964	Eudora Welty
1943–1946	No Contest	1965	Andrew Lytle
	during war	1966	W. D. Snodgrass
1947	Jesse Stuart	1967	James T. Farrell
1948	Katherine Anne	1968	Stanley Elkin
	Porter	1969	Theodore Weiss
1949	Mark Van Doren		

1970   SAUL BELLOW

Second, I should inform Bellow that he was the first choice of the faculty of the English Department (this must be the meaning of "empirically derived"), overwhelmingly elected to be our speaker in a poll conducted by Burke. Burke had begun by seeking nominations from members of the faculty, preparing from those nominations a ballot of forty-seven names, and submitting the ballot for faculty vote. In the final ballot Bellow's name led all the rest.

Thanks to a gratifying response by numerous colleagues, emeritus list-compilers, innocent bystanders, and a few sidewalk perverts, we now have a tentative but distinguished list of possible candidates for the guest speakership for the Literary Awards Banquet. As we prepare a negotiation list we must now go through the sad but necessary task of sorting out the inevitable bores, recluses, and basket cases to get a man of quality as well as reputation. If you have first-to-third-hand knowledge of noted authors who are able to talk as well as write, and liable to arrive in condition to do one or the other, it will be a service to us all if you will share your information.

We will try to engage the most distinguished writer first, subject of course to the foregoing kind of qualifications. While democracy can't work very efficiently where the electors can't be persuaded to vote and where the electees often can't be persuaded to serve, I will be grateful for any indications of preference or dispreference that you may be generous enough to offer. The present list should not be considered closed even though it must soon be reduced to manageability, since financial and logistic realities will surely bring about much of the reduction. So please don't be reticent about coming forward with names of other candidates.

> Thank you kindly,
> Joel Burke
> Literary Awards Committee

Saul Bellow	Archibald MacLeish
W. H. Auden	Wright Morris
Bernard Malamud	Richard Wilbur
Robert Lowell	James Dickey
J. F. Powers	Kenneth Cook
William Styron	Denise Levertov
Philip Roth	Reed Whittemore
James Purdy	John Updike
John Barth	Paul Bowles
Robert Penn Warren	John Ciardi
Peter Taylor	Walter Van Tilburg Clark
Irving Howe	Cleanth Brooks
Mark Schorer	Richard Ellmann
Stanley Kaufman	Kenneth Burke
Alfred Kazin	John Hawkes
Arthur Miller	Sol Yurick
Lionel Trilling	Norbert Duncan

Robert Coover	Mary McCarthy
Budd Schulberg	Richard Bissell
John Cheever	Leslie Fiedler
Edward Albee	Norman Mailer
John Aldridge	Truman Capote
Tennessee Williams	Tiffany Littlegreek Smith
Gore Vidal	

I was reluctant, I told Burke, to tell Bellow those things. I did not think they would be inducements. I understood Bellow well enough by now to anticipate the value he would place upon an election—"He did not care much for being *first* in the field." Disappointed to be ignored either by history or by Purdue University, yes. But if such a thing happened his genuine sadness would arise from his view of the event as but one of a succession of poor judgments, of which the world makes many.

Besides, I did not want Bellow to think I *thought* they were inducements. I was having troubles of my own with Bellow, my own relationship to keep in repair; my own identity; fragile, to be sure, but I had certain hopes for it. He was a goddam woodchuck, hard to corner, he wouldn't care to have as his biographer a man who believed we can *vote* for literary distinction. In 1965 Bellow had won a poll similar to the Purdue poll. Gordon Lloyd Harper, interviewing Bellow at that time, asked him whether the deaths of Faulkner and Hemingway had perhaps created a "vacuum in American letters, which we all know is abhorrent." Bellow replied: "Well, I don't know whether I would say a vacuum. Perhaps a pigeonhole. I agree that there is a need to keep the pigeonhole filled and that people are uneasy when there are vacancies. Also the mass media demand material—grist—and literary journalists have to create a major-league atmosphere in literature. The writers don't offer to fill the pigeonholes. It's the critics who want figures in the Pantheon. But there are many people who assume that every writer must be bucking for the niche. Why should writers wish to be rated—seeded—like tennis players? Handicapped like racehorses? What an epitaph for a novelist: 'He won all the polls'!"[1]

"Then, too," I said, "the insult of it all."

1. "Saul Bellow: An Interview," *The Paris Review*, Winter 1966, p. 55.

"I don't consider it an insult," said Burke, in the tone of our foot-ball debates, "for a man to be paid a thousand dollars just for stand-ing up and talking for thirty or forty minutes after a free meal."

"Just what you *said* is the insult," I said. Burke had omitted from his reckoning at least a quarter of a century of solitary labor, the wages of which were a thousand dollars and a free meal. Years of a gamble. So it was with boys at football, too, hundreds upon hun-dreds of boys practicing long darkening afternoons for every one boy who made it big on the Sunday television.

"I know it's not the thousand," said Professor Burke.

"The thousand is all it can possibly be," I said, "because the list of the past and the voting won't impress him. But I don't think I'm at liberty to chuck his thousand dollars in the street."

Show him the list of former speakers, said Burke. Tell him he won the balloting by a wide margin. "He'll come because of you," said Joel Burke.

"ARE YOU still at the airport?" Bellow asked.

"No," I replied, slightly laughing, "I'm down in West Lafayette," displeased with myself for saying "down," as if Chicago were "up."

"How's life?" he asked in a cheerful, receptive, outgoing tone.

"About as well as I can expect," I said.

"Then it's going pretty well," he said.

"I'm just a go-between here," I said.

"Going between what?" he asked.

There's nothing in this for me was what I meant, but of course there was. If he was the celebrated author of *Herzog* then I was the friend of the celebrated author. Hadn't I counted up the celebrated names 1928–1969 (some of them tarnished or faded now; one or two even whose spelling was in doubt) on Joel Burke's list and formed my own little sublist, subtotal, of the number of celebrated or semi-celebrated persons thereon whose lives my own had *personally* touched? Beside whom I had sat somewhere? To whom I had writ-ten a letter and received a reply? To whom I had talked on the tele-phone upon some inquiry or other? Happy, proud to be a part of American literature! And wasn't my own status inflated and ele-vated by my being sole agent of possibility, at least in the eyes of Professor Burke, in the matter of bringing to our campus and to our very Literary Awards Banquet table, an author so illustrious as Bel-

low, even as Burke's status was elevated by his being the sole cause
and agent of persuasion persuading *me* to persuade *Bellow*, even as
everyone else in the English Department would improve in standing
in his or her own eyes by being a guest at the banquet sitting however far from the celebrated author (whose newest novel, whether
one read it or not, was running now in the respected *Atlantic*)—all
of us improved by virtue of his having visited here and thereby al-
tered the character and image of Purdue University, to which one
belonged, even as one belonged to its technological fame or to its
athletic fame: distinction was distinction.

"Literary *awards* banquet," he said. He'd heard that word. Even if
he *accepted* the invitation, said Bellow, which he was not yet, this
moment, doing, he would need to be excused from sitting through
awards. He was to be excused, also, from any or all appearances on
radio or television, nor was he to be engaged in any interviews on
any kind of tape. "When is this, Mark?" he asked.

April.

"Then I'll have time to think it over," he said. "I want to clear my
head. Some things are bugging me. Legal and judicial things." These
things he would need to attend to before he could make a decision.
He'd be going to New York.

All right, how about if I called him again—say, December first?
That was the deadline Joel Burke had set.

No, said Bellow, he'd need more time than that—December
tenth, say.

Very well. Good. I would call him December tenth. I hoped that
that later date would not be objectionable to Burke.

"Why don't you come up to Chicago once in awhile," he asked,
"and fool around with Dick and me?"

"And end up in the Indiana dunes?" I said. "Let me read you
Burke's description," I said, returning to the business of my call. I
had before me Burke's memorandum on the subject, written with a
thin pen, no two letters touching. Other memoranda from Burke
during the course of these negotiations were sometimes written in
script, as if by a different hand. Why one, then the other? I never
knew. In Japan I never understood why a man wore *kimono* one day,
Western business suit the next. "Topic suggestions," I said, "morning address."

"Then actually there are *two* talks," Bellow said.

"I didn't realize that myself until this minute," I said.

"Well, go ahead," he said.

I paraphrased the following memorandum:

> Topic suggestions: (1) Morning address: your approach to your work, maybe something about the creative process. The Great Issues students will have been studying such things. (2) Evening address: Your choice, of course. Since the banquet is primarily for students who have won literary prizes you might well address yourself to the creative problems of the writer. Details & arrangements will be handled by Joel Burke of the English Dept., who is chairman of the Literary Awards Committee.

"The morning session," said Bellow, "would have to be just a bull session. I don't want to say the same thing over again. Free exchange in the morning session."

I assured him that that would be exactly proper, we needn't be as formal as Burke's memorandum directed. "I'm not in charge of all this," I said. "I'm only the telephone caller."

"Chester Eisinger's in charge," said Bellow.

"No," said I, "a young fellow. I've wondered, though, what you thought of Eisinger's section on you in his book."

Bellow replied with heat. "I never read that stuff. You don't *read* such stuff."

"Well, I read *Eisinger's*," I evasively said, "he's my colleague here." At that period of my life I did read "such things." I still to some extent respected critical writing, and I found it difficult to believe that Bellow read nothing that was written about him. By the time I was Bellow's age, however, I too saw how self-defeating it was to read of oneself. Somewhere I had turned a corner; no longer was Bellow difficult to believe on that subject.

"No radio stations," said Bellow. "No TV stations."

"No, no, of course not," I said.

"No, no, of course not," he replied, "but suddenly there were two speeches instead of one."

"Nothing between the morning and evening programs," I said.

"That's *right*," he said.

"Good," I said. Between morning and evening, if he accepted, I would guard him from exploitation. No free lectures. No free classroom appearances. No free interviews. No standing for photographs. No autographs. No manuscripts thrust into his hands. I would keep him to myself, free of everybody between morning and evening. Mark Rowan, who adored Bellow, would be lucky to get close enough to shake his hand. I would escort Bellow among hundreds of people without letting anyone meet him, lest the conservative author (so I then thought) of *Mr. Sammler's Planet*—victim at Columbia University, victim at San Francisco State, victim everywhere of the radicals trying to enlist him against the war in Vietnam—discover that his hopeful, aspiring, intended biographer, living for the moment at Purdue, was a leader of the rowdy radical mob.

ON THE tenth of December, as agreed, I telephoned Bellow at his apartment in Chicago, to hear his decision. At times past I had telephoned him on an appointed day only to discover that he was gone from home. He made no notes of such things—unless it were a note to unplug the phone. On this day, however, he answered at the first ring, appeared at leisure, unhurried, and we talked in a general way for two or three minutes. Soon he said, "I suppose you're calling about that . . ."

"Yes," I said, falling immediately into the language of a program chairman—"and everybody here is desperately hoping you'll come down and speak." Down!

"What date was that?" he asked. He didn't say Yes and he didn't say No. I told him the date, and he said, "I hope the air-conditioning and the P.A. work. They seldom work at the same time."

"Everything works at Purdue," I said.

"I want you to understand," he said, "I'm not doing this for the money."

I took this for Yes. I said, "You'll get a letter confirming everything from the fellow in charge."

"I'm doing it for you, Mark," he said. "I need the money like I need a hole in the head. It all goes for taxes. I'll use it to send my kid to camp," said Bellow, "though I don't approve of it. They spend all year with their peers, they should spend the summer with their parents." He seemed to be thinking out loud. "Enough people with their thumbprint on my windpipe," he said. After his talk, he said, he'd "continue on down to Crawfordsville." He had some family there; some connection.

"Ezra Pound went to college at Crawfordsville," I said. I had bad news to spring, and I stalled a little. "Have you been to New York?" I asked.

"I've been there and back. More than once. I've lost track."

"I feel," I said, warming up to my bad news, "that I've got to mention one change since we talked last month because I don't want any false pretenses. You know how they spring things on you after you get somewhere."

"What is it?" he inquired.

"I mentioned to you that the morning speech was to be very informal, questions and answers with twenty students, a small group, Great Issues, you remember?"

"Let's hope that the issues are very great and the group is very small," he said.

"That's what I was hoping," I said, "because that's what I was told, but now Burke tells me that at the morning session there will actually be six hundred students."

"Good God," he said, "you can't have very much Q. and A. with that large a group."

"That's what I've been thinking," I said.

"But I can handle it," Bellow said.

"You can still cancel if you like," I said. "They told you twenty and zoomed to six hundred . . ."

"I can *handle* it, Mark," saying again, "I'm doing it for *you*," proving that Joel Burke knew better than I the way of these alliances, these closed systems: unknown to myself, I was of a fraternity, of a monolith. A few days later Professor Burke issued a confident memorandum to all members of the English Department:

> 'Tis the week before Christmas and a happy time to announce that with the kind and able help of Professor Harris we have managed to secure Saul Bellow as the guest speaker for the Literary Awards Banquet. I hope the choice is approved by your attendance (April 30th). Those who know Mr. Bellow assure me that his speaking ability is commensurate with his distinguished reputation as a novelist, so I think we can look forward to a good evening.
>
> Merry Christmas
> Joel Burke
> Literary Awards Committee

As THE TIME approached for Bellow's visit to Purdue, Professor Burke was eager to assist in every possible way. He had written a letter to Bellow, but he had not received a reply. He therefore asked me if I would follow up his inquiry by telephone, covering questions he had organized in his customary systematic fashion on his customary yellow paper lined with blue, this time in curling, connected script:

BELLOW
(1) Did he get the Burke letter as to time schedule?
    (a) Great Issues 10:30 AM, Loeb Playhouse, before 600? people interested in creativity
    (b) Banquet, 7:00 PM, North Ballroom, PMU. More formal talk before roughly 200 people.
(2) Travel plans—pick up at airport? Time? Lodgings—stay overnight or not—do you want a reservation? where?
(3) Reception, cocktail party before the lecture? (c. 5:30?) Hosted by Chet Eisinger?
(4) Anything else we can manage to do for you? (Contact Joel Burke)
(We have the publicity material from your publisher)

Promptly I agreed to follow up. For a biographer, every moment of living relationship with his or her subject is precious.

On the other hand, *Life* magazine had just appeared with the article about him by Jane Howard, author of *Please Touch*. For several days after reading it I did not care if Bellow came to Purdue. She spoke of Bellow as one who "distrusts those of his colleagues who assume 'defiant, radical, independent points of view' for what he thinks are the wrong reasons. 'A radical stance,' he says, 'is the ultimate luxury for those who already have everything else.'" Of "campus revolutionaries" Bellow said, in a talk at Yale, "The trouble with the destroyers is that they're just as phoney as what they've come to destroy. Maybe civilization *is* dying, but it still exists, and meanwhile we have our choice: we can either rain more blows on it, or try to redeem it."

This was not a new view of Bellow's, but its public nature in *Life* embarrassed me in the commons room, where the word "stance" was sometimes employed to suggest insincerity on the part of the anti-Vietnam professors.

The article also raised some troubled thoughts in the minds of Joel Burke and others whose stake was large in the success of the annual banquet. Howard opened her article with a view of Bellow at Yale. She emphasized his distaste for public appearance. Worse, the students found him both hostile and dull. It was a bad advertisement, no boost to ticket sales. "Yet there he was, lured to edify the promising young. There he sat captive, donnishly tweedy, physically slight and boyish despite his white hair and 54 years. And there they sat, long-haired, languid and oddly unresponsive. . . . 'Well,' he said, 'I see I've reduced you all to silence.' More silence. 'Well,' he said, 'it's late and I have an early train to catch.' It wasn't late at all; it was only 9 o'clock, but the group dispersed. 'Ah well,' said Bellow as he shrugged on his imposing sheepskin-lined coat, 'they and I don't talk the same language.'" Stilted photography—Bellow, in collar and tie, smiles in the most unnatural way at Daniel, then six, who is thinking of something else. "Though his three sons all live in different cities, Bellow is an attentive father."

For several days I called him without being able to reach him. At last, on April 26, he answered my call. The sound of his voice restored me to my sense of his best self, of Bellow a good deal more complicated than Jane Howard or anyone could make him within the limits of *Life*; of Bellow the author of *Seize the Day*, which I was then reading with a group of Master's candidates. I was also reading galleys of *The Goy*, but I did not mention that title to him. "Hello, Mark," he cheerily said, but his voice was clogged, as if he were choking. How was he? Fine, he said. He didn't *sound* fine. The Literary Awards Banquet was four days away. If Bellow were sick Burke would die. "Just a frog in my throat," he said.

Did he receive Burke's letter?

"Burke who?" he asked. No, he did not. What letter?

A schedule of the arrangements, said I, Great Issues, questions about travel plans, cocktail party.

"What's this Great Issues group?" Bellow asked.

"Well, I mentioned it way back in December," I said. "You remember there were twenty people inflated to six hundred."

"What great issues do they discuss?" he asked. "I don't want to go in there in my astronaut suit."

"You don't want to be set upon like Mr. Sammler. I understand."

"I shouldn't be put into a shock box," Bellow said, experimenting with a few metaphors. "I'm not being *punished* for something. I shouldn't be put on display like Eichmann in Jerusalem. I shouldn't be a clay pipe in a shooting gallery. It shouldn't be death row. The university should protect me from that." Earlier he had written: "There is a taste for Roman holidays, for bloody entertainment, in universities and intellectual circles. Novelists and poets are prodded into gladiatorial fights. Literature is acquiring a sporting color, like hockey or prize fighting. Editors of literary magazines or professors who arrange a visiting lecture or annual symposium often behave like fight promoters. I have more than once been invited by Professor X to confront Professor Y who has called me (the text is usually quoted) a sellout, a flunkey, a faker, or a fink. The invitation reads, 'I am sure you would like an opportunity to reply to this from the same platform, in public.'"[2]

"I guarantee you," I replied, "that I'll investigate this whole thing and see that you are protected."

"Instead of six hundred students they should let me speak to a hundred as a reward for their *A*s and *B*s," said Bellow.

"My understanding is that you're not in a situation in which confrontations occur," I said. "It's a class, a regular class."

"But it might," he said. "SDS will get wind of it. It'll be placarded all over the place."

It had not been placarded. "They don't placard a *class*," I said.

"No placards?" he asked.

"At least I haven't seen any," I replied—I was too busy taking my "radical stance," I might have replied, too busy with the "ultimate luxury" of opposing the war in Vietnam; it might not be a bad idea to placard a little myself here and there, and call my placards to the attention of my friends in Students for a Democratic Society in case they hadn't seen them. Oh, they'd see them!

"You and I are experienced men," said Bellow, "we know how these things happen."

"I'll be sure it won't happen," I said.

At some point in our conversation I mentioned my trip to Chicago earlier that month with my son Anthony. I assured him that I had

2. *The Arts and the Public*, ed. James E. Miller, Jr., and Paul D. Herring (Chicago: University of Chicago Press, 1967), p. 17.

tried him on the telephone. On that trip I had had the rotten experience of being held up on a city bus: a black fellow had tried to steal my wrist watch. I resisted, he fled. Bellow asked, "Did he have a weapon?" It was the question everyone asked. "No," I said, "and he didn't show me his penis, either"—an allusion to an action in *Mr. Sammler's Planet* notable for its vividness and its passion coolly related. "You were lucky," said Bellow.

"Now," said I, "cocktail party at the Eisingers'. This exceeds the original agreement. You don't have to accept it if you don't want to." A cocktail party worried me. There, if anywhere, people might mention my antiwar politics. "I'll back you up on that," I said.

"No, gladly," he said. "I like Chester very much. I like to get plastered ahead of time."

"Travel plans," I said. "Pick up at airport?" Here our conversation started downward.

He said he would be bringing with him a dear friend who would drive him back to Chicago if he were "too drunk" to do so himself, or they might go on to Cincinnati to some sort of family function there. Or he *might* fly. He asked me about roads—how long to drive from Chicago to Lafayette?—but he never permitted me to answer his question. "I'll be driving down Wednesday," he said, "and driving back Thursday night."

"Not going to Cincinnati then," I said.

"I've changed my mind about Cincinnati."

"Or Crawfordsville?" I asked.

No, he had changed his mind about Crawfordsville, too.

"I'll make reservations for you at the Student Union," I said.

"Not the Union," he said, "that'll be too noisy."

"Then I'll make a reservation at the Campus Inn," I said, switching from the plural to the singular, for I did not know at this point whether he had also changed his mind about his dear friend. I hoped not. The Campus Inn was a motel on the highway entering town, and I asked him, "How shall I make the reservation? For how many?"

Angrily, deeply annoyed, he said, "One room."

I had done the single thing I wished above all to avoid; pried into his business, stamped my thumbprint on his windpipe; crowded him. Was my curiosity relevant? Or was I prying? Was I gathering gossip for my biography? Yet I felt that I was seeking legitimate information. "One room," I said. "One person? Two people?"

"Just take it in my name and I'll sign it," he said, sarcastically adding, "You must have registered at a motel some time in your life."

"Yes, but not for someone else," I said. A man of experience I may have been, but this was a little new.

"They don't have to know all the details," he said.

I was chagrined, sheepish. I was left with a bad taste which lingered for hours. I felt that I had intruded upon him, that I had been indiscreet, certainly less than my best self. A sophisticated biographer would have engaged one room without a word. Nobody had to know all the details.

Chapter Eight

BELLOW CAME and went. Years afterward, the image of his presence I remembered best, vividest, was a lady, Helen Wollan, wife of Gerhard Wollan, professor of mathematics, on the sidewalk, in the humid night, five minutes after Bellow's address—a lovely, kind, generous woman of good will, friend to young people, friend to peace, contributor, contributive—expressing to me in the clearest terms her extreme displeasure with Bellow's address to the Literary Awards Banquet, just concluded. "Culture Now: Some Animadversions, Some Laughs." That was Bellow's title. She had got the animadversions, but not the laughs.

She had left, as I had, before the awarding of the prizes, not to pursue me, I think, though now that she had me she'd tell me her fury. It was bad, that was all, bad, bad, that was all she could say. It was all bad. Terrible. It was awful. She meant by that, as other people would in the days following, that it was tedious, inscrutable, mysterious, difficult, and finally affronting.

"I thought it was challenging," I said. It addressed itself to issues still unfamiliar. True, it wasn't precisely entertaining—some people seemed to have expected that twenty-five years of labor should produce an hour's light comedy, one-liners, juggling, magic. "He said things people don't dare to say," I said. "Wasn't anything *nice* about it?"

"It was all bad," she said, speaking in a fiery fashion I had never heard from her, nor ever expected—"all bad, and a little bit nice."

"I agree with the last part of what you said," said a gentleman standing beside me. "The niceness."

Mrs. Wollan was shocked to see that everything she had said she had said in the presence of Bellow himself, the gentleman beside me, whom she now gradually recognized in the gloom, in the steaming night, as the speaker of the evening, earlier seen from a distant table, but she retracted nothing, nor withdrew a single syllable, but only herself withdrew, striding into the night. I never saw her again.

Summoned to speak the world's language from a platform, Bellow followed the form ("Evening address . . . you might well address yourself to the creative problems of the writer") while defying gentility. If he was going to say something he was going to *say* something. That was his radicalism—not to retreat from his aesthetic conviction even to please the crowd. He was Bummidge beyond entertainment. He had said from another platform that morning that he'd not be gladiator, either. He was an artist or conscientious worker, bringing to our assembly his work composed alone at the best level of his meditation. He had prepared his lesson. If we insisted with torrents of mail upon paying him a thousand dollars for bringing his meditation into the open he'd take it. But he'd do his thing, as the saying was, not *ours*: he had not offered himself nor even really wanted to come, neither for the money nor the friendship. But when he did come it was his person who came, it was who he was, not some genial man but the earnest work, reading aloud, quite as if it were Tivoli with his hat on.

In the tedium, in the difficulty, in the airless heat, not everyone was disappointed. Not all faces fell. For myself, I had begun to understand him: that we made the world safe by a deepening aesthetic devotion rendering our obscenity unacceptable to ourselves. Only art and education could overcome barbarism. "You don't found universities in order to destroy culture. For that you want a Nazi party."

Elsewhere in the Purdue Memorial Union, on that night, at that very hour, students and other people were watching Richard Nixon, then president, announcing on television that our warplanes were resuming the bombing of North Vietnam, and extending the war to Cambodia. By morning America had entered a new phase of its domestic war against its warmakers. On this night, however, Bellow denounced not the war but certain literary persons—notably William Phillips of *Partisan Review*, and Leslie Fiedler in *Playboy*—

who seemed to him to represent a popular state of mind in America not less dangerous than the mind of the warmaker.

> I have spoken with brilliant young men, leaders of the New Left, who decline to say what they will do when they take power. Now literature and painting have made me familiar with action theory. "How do I know what I think till I see what I say?" asked E. M. Forster. But do we want aesthetic methods in politics? Revolutionary improvisation does not attract me. Can one seriously discuss a movement which will not disclose its plan for a new social order? Even Mr. Phillips seems to be aware of the danger of this. "In general," he says, "perhaps an even more important problem is that unless one has some general idea of the kind of society one would like to see and of the forces working to create it, he tends to go for *any* militant act and *any* radical doctrine, the more militant and radical the better. The result is to transform a tactic into an end, converting politics into a game in which the new radicals trump the old ones." Riot, arson, bombing do not suggest any sort of game to me.[1]

How were war and revolution different? Killing was killing. Mr. Sammler had known it for what it was. "He knew it was one of the luxuries. No wonder princes had for so long reserved the right to murder with impunity. . . . Sammler thought that this was what revolutions were really about. In a revolution you took away the privileges of an aristocracy and redistributed them. What did equality mean? Did it mean all men were friends and brothers? No, it meant that all belonged to the elite. Killing was an ancient privilege. This was why revolutions plunged into blood. Guillotines? Terror? Only a beginning—nothing. There came Napoleon, a gangster who washed Europe well in blood. There came Stalin, for whom the really great prize of power was unobstructed enjoyment of murder. That mighty enjoyment of consuming the breath of men's nostrils, swallowing their faces like a Saturn. This was what the conquest of power really seemed to mean. Sammler tied his shoelaces—continued dressing."

1. "Culture Now: Some Animadversions, Some Laughs," *Modern Occasions*, Winter 1971, pp. 166–67.

AS USUAL, not even the simplest connection with Bellow could be completed without complication. He was to have arrived at the Campus Inn at 10:00 P.M. He was early. When I called the Campus Inn precisely at that hour I was told that he was no longer in his room. Josephine and I drove there, thinking he might have gone to the bar. He was nowhere. I telephoned home, reaching my son Anthony just as he was stepping into the shower (he'd not have heard my ring a minute later, with embarrassing consequences). He told me that Bellow had called to say he had gone to the Eisingers'. Anthony described him as "gruff."

In the warm evening in the Eisingers' cool living-room we found Bellow and his dear friend, a woman of thirty-five or forty years old, mother of two children whom she had not brought with her. She worked for a notable magazine which was then in the process of changing its name from something with the word "Bulletin" in its title to something without. She was neither voluptuous like Bonne Amie nor vivacious like Miss Stat. Bellow wore a T-shirt emphasizing his sturdy chest. I recalled his chest from the moment of his admitting me to his apartment that October Sunday morning. His face was now more markedly lined. When he smiled, his pattern of wrinkles and creases leaped to life, as if the natural state of his face was an expression of happiness—a bit red this evening, however, perhaps from the drive from Chicago. That, and the bright cherry tie he wore all the following day, gave him an appearance of color in spite of his being mainly gray: gray hair, gray three-hundred-dollar Italian suit—"Heartbroken, and gussied up, with my Italian pants and my fountain pens, and my grief," poor Herzog. Josephine wished I cared for clothes, as Bellow did. In my presence he was (wonderful word from *Humboldt's Gift*) a "contrast-gainer."

Eisinger, too, was a striking man, slender and tall, but round-shouldered as if the result of his humble intention to bring himself down, lower, closer to us smaller men. His thought was clear, his speech powerful and eloquent: he could address a meeting all the more persuasively for a sympathetic treble to his voice. So-called creative people inspired him. He once told me I turned him on, so to speak, but when it came to the practical matter of department politics he saw I was no help. Writing of Bellow, he could respect Bellow's distinction between "the order that ideas have" and the "unknown process of the imagination,"[2] but he did not abandon himself to intuitive or impulsive processes; so that when, at the end, introducing Bellow to the banquet, Eisinger, filled with emotion, sought to describe so fine a writer, his language was unequal to his feeling: he oddly hinted that the worth of a writer might be measured by the number of books written *about* him by critics and scholars; tumbling into superlatives—Bellow "our finest writer"— sacrificing his best everyday eloquence to his public excitement; strangely rational, controlled. As if criticism were a science!

We were six in the Eisingers' living-room. Tomorrow we would be one hundred in the same room for cocktails and gossip before the banquet. I sat beside Bellow. Then he rose and sat facing me, as if to see me better. Often, when I spoke, he appeared to be especially attentive, tilting his head flatteringly to one side to give me his full ear. I wondered if he was considering me as his biographer. Not much had lately been said of that project—a little by me and none at all by him. I had now read beyond doubt everything he had published, I was "teaching" one book of his each semester, and I was devising on 3×5 cards a little retrieval system for noteworthy facts or literary passages I could imagine myself quoting in the happy event that I ever actually started to write his biography. I had notes suggesting research—*speak to Dolly, she knew him in Paris* and *find out if Schorer is Jewish.*

I had read so thoroughly in Bellow that our meeting was now a kind of anticlimax. Why should anyone care to *see* this gray man who could *read* him? This question began to be real to me. This Bellow was only an outer person, tomorrow's speaker, the department guest, nobody special, neither he nor his lady. Who were they? Visibly ordinary. He was somebody whose name I would have forgotten. Don't you remember, we met him once at the Eisingers? He was witty, but many men and women were wittier of speech, quicker, faster, more rapid-tongued. Of course, their truth of speech was lost upon the air. Genius is wit organized. Bellow in the flesh spoke tentatively, one moment precisely, another moment off the top of his head, stream-of-consciousness, spurting words, careless, bouncing

2. *Fiction of the Forties* (Chicago: University of Chicago Press, 1963), p. 344.

sounds. He yielded few gems along the way. He would revise, organize. This ordinary man one met in the Eisingers' living-room was
perhaps a writer, it seemed so from what one had heard of writers'
reticence, their slow speech.

Josephine mentioned *Mr. Sammler's Planet*, which she had just
read. A student had recently written about it on a doctoral examination in Modern *British*. Eisinger mentioned to Bellow that *Seize the
Day* was read by all students for the master's degree examination. "I
thought I was writing books," said Bellow, "not examinations." He
seemed displeased that people were reading his work in that way—
to be tested upon it. Josephine had recently sent letters to several
authors on the question, "How does a writer begin?" All the authors
had answered but Bellow. He said he had not received her letter, but
he would answer it now. "A writer begins because he is moved," said
Bellow. "He reads. Abraham Lincoln was one of America's greatest
writers. We should tear down the universities and put up log
cabins."

Professor Eisinger mentioned the long history of the Literary
Awards Banquets, touching upon memorable moments. For example, Katherine Anne Porter (1948) stopped her address in mid-sen-
tence, refusing to continue, when she noticed the Dean asleep
beside her at table. She descended from the platform, strode through
the astonished crowd, out the door, and to her room at the Union
where she remained drinking for five days. When Dreiser came
(1936) he had with him *two* women.

Bellow compared the characters of Porter and Dreiser, offering the
opinion that a writer is fortunate if his "problem" is sex rather than
liquor: for writing, said Bellow, is a sensual act, the writer is a sen-
sualist; therefore the writer whose vice is sensuality can be com-
forted with the idea that he is all of a consistency. I said I was glad I
was no drinker. Bellow asked me if I expected to see Mark Schorer
often in California. "He's trying to imitate Fitzgerald," said Bellow,
"who drank himself to death."

"I thought Schorer's biography of Sinclair Lewis was awfully
good," I said. "I wrote him a letter."

"Certainly," said Bellow, "Lewis also drank himself to death." He
added: "Schorer is one of those Jews who has tried to escape into the
established culture."

"Schorer is *Jewish*?" I exclaimed, astonished.

"There you are," said Bellow.

"Herzog also tried to escape into the established culture," I said.

"But he didn't succeed," Bellow replied.

Both Bellow and the Eisingers had recently traveled to Africa. Bellow, of course, had written of Africa long before he had seen it. On his recent trip he had been "excited" by a crocodile in "the White Nile," carrying that memory forward into his amazing story, "A Silver Dish," in 1978.

> It was this: On a launch near the Murchison Falls in Uganda, he had seen a buffalo calf seized by a crocodile from the bank of the White Nile. . . . The parent buffaloes couldn't figure it out. Under the water the calf still threshed, fought, churned the mud. Woody, the robust traveler, took this in as he sailed by, and to him it looked as if the parent cattle were asking each other dumbly what had happened. He chose to assume that there was pain in this, he read brute grief into it.[3]

Word of Africa reminded me that my landlord, a nuclear engineer, had told me only that day that he had been reading *Henderson the Rain King* but feeling like Portnoy of *Portnoy's Complaint*. "He doesn't know whether to travel or masturbate," said Bellow. I asked him if he remembered a woman Portnoy in *Herzog*, or a man named Moses Herzog in Joyce's *Ulysses*, but he did not remember either.

Astoundingly, Bellow condemned my friend Blau for having "missed it . . . blown it" at Lincoln Center, in New York. "He shouldn't have been so ambitious," Bellow said. "He should have begun with a couple of easy plays before going so far out."

"You didn't write easy novels," I argued, "before getting on to serious work. Blau brought stupid New York down on his head with an *antirevolution play*. Your position exactly." It seemed to me that Bellow had not drawn the right conclusion from the "failure" on Broadway of *The Last Analysis*. Years later, in *Humboldt's Gift*, Citrine's play, *Von Trenck*, "ran for eight months on Broadway," and earned for Citrine eight thousand dollars a week. But it had been corrupted, reduced to meaninglessness: "I had the attention of the

3. *The New Yorker*, September 25, 1978, p. 40.

public for nearly a year, and I taught it nothing." Then what was the point of succeeding? Blau had refused to surrender his artistic conviction.

Once more Bellow denounced Blau's prose. "Maybe when you get down there to his school in southern California he'll teach you how to read it," he said.

"I already *can* read it," I said. "Blau's writing is *associational.*"

"Too much so," said Bellow.

"Frost speaks of *feats of association,*" I said.

"Blau should bring it under control," said Bellow.

"It's really quite marvelous," I said.

"I'd rather take a prostate examination," said Bellow.

While he was arguing with me about Blau he was arguing another question with Marjorie Eisinger. He was an old-time movie hero fighting off two enemies at once. I overheard Marjorie say, "I refuse to blame everything on young people." I was hoping to avoid arguing activist politics with Bellow. I did not think he would want an activist biographer. But the Eisingers had no such reluctance. We spoke of the Indiana primary campaign of Toal for Congress. Toal was the peace candidate. An argument against Toal was that he could not win. I said I intended to vote for him nonetheless—if we won with the wrong candidate, what had we won? It sounded, I think, more like idealism and innocence than activist politics. I thought it might counteract anything Bellow was likely to hear about me at the cocktail party tomorrow. "I refuse to lose my innocence," I said.

"You won't," said Bellow. I think he thought it a sign of my innocence that I taught "creative writing." He had many doubts about such a scheme. He said, "I'm sick and tired of the progressive-school approach to writing—let's all put down our baseball gloves and write a poem." I said I hoped he would not devote his speeches tomorrow to a public attack on the credibility of my teaching. It seemed to me, I said, that students who try to write become ultimately more respectful of literature than students who dive right into the swamp of criticism. I said I thought a critical confusion existed between the order ideas have and the process of the imagination—paraphrasing Professor Eisinger, with whom I had mildly debated this issue.

True, said Bellow, ideas are "not explicit" in his own work. I thought this was good for Eisinger to hear, but whether he related it to his own critical procedures I do not know. If he did, he did not look upon it as the nullification of his life's work—he did not rush into the other room and shoot himself.

Shortly after midnight Josephine and I drove Bellow and his dear friend to the Campus Inn, parting from them with plans for meeting in the morning.

ASSISTANT PROFESSOR Joel Burke, chairman of the Literary Awards Banquet committee, was to have met us the following morning at the Campus Inn at ten o'clock, but he did not appear. We waited for him. Then we went on without him to the Loeb Theater, where, just before Bellow stepped onstage, Burke joined him to tell him that he would be unable to attend Bellow's morning talk because he had "business." He did not say what business. Since December, Burke had been engaged in organizing Bellow's April day, but now that the day had come the business of it all was carrying Burke away. "Feffer was gone, had been called away to the telephone."

Driving that morning from the Campus Inn to the Loeb Theater we passed a fraternity house where young men were playing ball barechested on the lawn. "The fraternity boys have big breasts," said Bellow, "they should be in a sorority." Men with womanly breasts are a phenomenon observed several times in Bellow's fiction. Bellow asked to see the house of Bill Gass, the writer, in whose work he apparently had some interest: he had once given Gass an award in a literary competition. I slowed the car as we passed Gass's house. Bellow commented especially on its southern colonial pillars, as if they were meaningful, seeming to suggest that Gass, like Ellison perhaps, chose to imagine himself a landed gentleman. On the other hand, I cautiously replied, revealing my favorable feeling toward Gass, he was an anti-Vietnam-War radical, famous at Purdue for reading his work aloud to students, rallying them with his more or less puzzling prose in which young people saw a deep meaning I did not personally see.

Some years afterward I discovered that I had slowed my car before the wrong house. Poor Bellow! His whole speculation was predicated on my error. Gass's house was plain brick, no pillars, and Gass

himself may or may not therefore have been that cluster of contra-
dictions to which Bellow was sensitive in other writers; contradic-
tion was the characteristic common to American writers yearning
for everything, being everything to everybody, southern gentleman,
academic radical, Whitmanian singer (but subtler); where art and
wealth both lay within reach American writers tried for both, often
smashing-up in the process. Little wonder that Lewis and Fitzgerald
were on Bellow's mind. For *Humboldt's Gift* certain thoughts on
the course of literary career were settling into place. In Humboldt
"all his desires were contradictory. He wanted to be magically and
cosmically expressive and articulate, able to say *anything*; he
wanted also to be wise, philosophical, to find the common ground of
poetry and science, to prove that the imagination was just as potent
as machinery, to free and to bless humankind. But he was also out to
be rich and famous. And of course there were the girls. Freud himself believed that fame was pursued for the sake of the girls. But
then the girls were pursuing something themselves." Gass had gone
off with a younger woman. At the Eisingers' cocktail party that afternoon Bellow asked me to point out Gass's estranged wife, Mary
Pat, and he went to her to talk.

I had difficulty finding a parking space. Bellow complained that
special provision should be made for faculty; where faculty was concerned he was rather caste-minded, petulant, peevish, especially
when he was inconvenienced. He seemed to feel that someone
should always be handy to assist him. At last I found a space. I was
short coins. Bellow gave me some silver, which I tried to repay him
later, which he declined to accept, and which reminded me of my
experience at a conference in Dedham, Massachusetts, of seeking a
nickel for five pennies, to make a telephone call. Ralph Ellison was
standing talking to a man I did not know. The man gave me a nickel.
I tried to press my pennies into his hand, but he resisted. Ellison
smiled at my innocence—the man upon whom I was forcing my
pennies was Edwin Land, the Polaroid billionaire. Bellow said, "Bil-
lionaires are different from us."

Walking from the parking meter we instantly encountered William Stafford, editor of the esteemed journal *Modern Fiction Studies*, to whom I introduced Bellow and his dear friend. I was very fond
of Stafford. But then and afterward, when I linked his magazine to

the idea of Bellow, all I could think of was its reference to a fine essay of Bellow's as a "tirade against symbol-searchers."[4] More and more I could understand Bellow's cringing at the sound of literary criticism, the more I studied him the more I myself cringed, felt besieged; more and more I could see his search for privacy as less an eccentricity than a necessity. We walked with Stafford across the Mall where, not many days earlier, the students (and some professors) had massed, encamped against the war. Tonight, after the news of Cambodia, they would renew their mortal struggle, and I would rejoice at their irreverence, their harassing and insulting spokesmen of the establishment, defenders of the war; and I in the commons room would renew my shouting and screaming and swearing at Mark Rowan, whom I now saw for the first time this day spying Bellow at a distance, too respectful to approach, circling, wishing, gazing with a smile on tiptoe at this man whose work with love and comprehension he had read and admired for twenty years, who would have dashed forward at the merest signal to embrace the man who had brought him so much pleasure and enlightenment in a life devoted to books, learning, reading (all the while smoking himself to death). But I gave him no signal. No signal was mine to give. It was Bellow, not I, as everyone knew, who had specifically required, as a condition of his coming, that he be left to his privacy. From my car to the stage of Loeb Theater I escorted Bellow through hundreds of people without his meeting any but Stafford. Had it not been for the Eisingers' cocktail party that afternoon he would have met almost no one all day.

In Loeb Theater were several hundred students and faculty. Great Issues. Swarming with critics at all levels of their education. Bellow sat on a chair onstage beneath blazing lights. I was to introduce him—a lovely assignment passed to me after four months of planning only that morning (before I was out of bed), by Dr. Huston, director of the course in Great Issues. Dr. Huston seemed to think I was in charge of it all. No, no, Joel Burke was in charge. I saw that people thought it was my party. I was Mayor Naftalin on the twenty-fifth floor.

4. "Patterns of Rebirth in *Henderson the Rain King,*" *Modern Fiction Studies,* Winter 1966/67, p. 413.

Luckily, my research was all in my head, this was somebody whom (I said) I introduced with unqualified pleasure, he had liberated me, he had sped up my maturity, he had made me want to write better, I could recite his books in the perfect chronological order I had read them. At one point I interrupted myself to ask whether the hot lights of the stage might be extinguished, I thought it discourteous to a visitor to blind him and broil him. From the darkness someone called invisibly back that the lights could not be lowered— "This is being taped." Yet the promise had been that Bellow was not to be on any tape. The great institution of technology could neither lower the lights nor cool them. Nobody could move. Orders could not be retracted. The war begun could not be stopped. Four months of planning had gone into this! I did not protest further. And I learned years later, assembling my facts to write this book, that if any film had been made of Bellow onstage at Loeb Theater nobody knew where it was. Made and destroyed. Made and lost. Made and misplaced. Misfiled. Yet the lights were scorching hot, and I slipped out from under them, offstage, to the sound of the friendliest applause for the central figure.

This was by agreement not a prepared speech but a question-and-answer session. The topic of Great Issues at this point of the semester was Man and the Imagination. "I am the animal," said Bellow, "not the zoologist." Nevertheless he would try to describe the place of the imaginative writer. He would give us a little historical essay.

The writer has always been "the literate explainer." Clergymen and poets of the nineteenth century taught moral lessons. They were instructive and uplifting. They taught people how to live. They surveyed the known world, comprehending all branches of human knowledge.

Then came America and the American West, and that was a new world, yet to be known and surveyed. "*Real* men," said Bellow, were no longer poets or clergymen—"Real men were out biting other people's necks." Here he supplied a long series of images I was able only partially to keep up with—guns, ropes, jeeps, bullfights, whiskey bottles—items of American manhood all finally ironically equated with "taming the land."

Having lost the position of literate explainers, writers now sought respect by becoming men of action, men of power, defining manhood and then living by their own definition. From Whitman to

Hemingway they provided the image: style, virility, courage, taciturnity. Here again was Humboldt in the making, foolish, rough, tough poet, destroying that part of himself which Charlie Citrine, on the other hand, values: the learned life, sobriety, the old system. Citrine, opening his *Times* on the 727 jet from New York to Chicago, reads the obituary of his friend, his one-time mentor and idol, Humboldt, "dead in a dismal hotel off Times Square. I, a different sort of writer, remained to mourn him in prosperity out in Chicago."

A question from the floor. I could not hear it. We can guess it. Bellow's answer: "The writer who has influenced me most is God. The Bible. I was a little mixed up about the style. At eight when I was in a hospital a kind Christian lady brought me a copy of the New Testament. I read that the Jews had been responsible for the death of Christ—except me, of course, I was in the hospital." All his life Herzog carried a memory of the kind Christian lady, her button shoes, her hatpin "projected from the back of her head like a trolley rod." But Herzog calls her "goyische," somehow a bad lady, in spite of her kindness to him. (On the following day, at my house, when I showed him the jacket design for my book, *The Goy*, he turned away in displeasure when he saw that I had not changed the title.)

I do not know how, in view of Bellow's remarks, people at that morning session of Great Issues could have thought him mindlessly patriotic. Perhaps some people had not come to listen, for I felt the stirrings of debate even before he was drawn upon grounds where to speak his true feeling was to invite debate. Bellow slowly rephrased a question someone had asked from the floor. He hesitated. Why fight? Have a nice day. "Is the avant-garde writer a member of the avant-garde?" Essentially, he replied, no. A great many people are dressed up to look like the avant-garde, but they are not the avant-garde. The genuine avant-garde—well, that was something else. Looking for the avant-garde, he said, most people look to the wrong place. It was the heart of the problem. People confuse "art-behavior" with art. "A radical in politics," he said—here causing a rising muttering and grumbling, a stirring in the hall—"is not known by his dress but by his inner thought, courageous action. America is a great country for putting all things into reverse: my mother wanted me to be clean, so I'll be filthy. It's like the man in Chicago running off to the brothel: 'The Tribune is against syphilis so I'm for it.'"

He had been got to. He was debating now. *The romantic asser-tions of independence are herd phenomena,* he said, *people who demonstrate themselves.* "I dislike public display. I never wanted to assume leadership. This is becoming a gladiatorial show"—this readiness for confrontation, this mob, this herd, and Bellow the tar-get beneath the lights—"and many writers like to offer themselves to the gladiatorial show. They like to vie with the entertainment in-dustry. Some writers write only long enough to qualify for public life. The *writer* works in isolation."

Another question. Bellow replied calmly. "When I hear this word 'obsolescence' I cringe a little bit. A 'dearth of ideas' in novels, you say? A dearth of ideas for one person is too many ideas for someone else. . . . This demand for heightened stimulation: Toqueville said that people would demand ever stronger stimulants. It would reach a point of frenzy. Literature can't compete with the orgy. Boredom increases as excitement increases. It's the function of the news to destroy tranquility. All events come to you, asking you, 'What are you going to do about it?' The individual has the megalomaniacal feeling of boundless importance and influence. If he's had 'sen-sitivity training' I don't see how he can bear it all."

Not he, but they, perhaps were obsolete, stimulated, manipulated, and thereby rendered ineffective. The hour was almost ended, and the possibility for conflict certainly so by the introduction of a most civilized question, this from Sister Joan Grumman, a Catholic nun, soon thereafter resigned from her order. She asked about the theol-ogy of *Seize the Day.* I caught only a part of Bellow's reply. He said, "Even idiots tell you the truth nowadays." She referred to Dr. Tam-kin in that book. "A plausible phoney," Bellow replied, "a deep pho-ney. That's not the worst way to be deep."

DUE TO a bureaucratic misunderstanding we were not at first ad-mitted for lunch to the Sagamore Room of the Union. The reser-vation had been made for "Great Issues." We mistakenly called ourselves "English Department." When we were at last admitted we sat in two rows at a long table—Professors Burke, Eisinger, Harris, and Hayman of English, Huston and Hatheway of history; Bellow, his dear friend; an unidentified male person; and a black-bearded teaching assistant named Tuck, an Arkansan, for whom literary theory was more pressing than hunger. Bellow, for whom it was not, ate corned beef and cabbage.

Tuck wished immediately to know the answer to the secret nobody can fathom: *exactly* what is the relationship between the author of a novel and its hero or narrator? It was not a new accusation—"You hide behind your characters with your filthy ideas," said my Minneapolis friend. "Why didn't you name Herzog—Bellows?" somebody said in San Francisco. There the fight began. I felt that Tuck was honestly inquiring. He did not yet know that the question was unanswerable—he did not then believe that *any* question was unanswerable. "For example," said Tuck, "I was glancing last night at *Henderson the Rain King*."

"You were glancing at it," Bellow said.

"Yes, and what is the author's responsibility for the statements of the narrator?" Tuck asked.

"Henderson is a comic convention," said Bellow.

"Henderson was *inconsistent*," said Tuck.

"He's entitled to be whatever he was," said Bellow, addressing himself with cast-down eyes to his corned beef and cabbage.

"Were you inconsistent yourself?" Tuck asked.

Bellow perfectly replied, "Well, perhaps I shouldn't have written it. Perhaps it was a mistake."

"What kind of criticism do you prefer?" Tuck asked.

"Criticism of a high order," Bellow replied.

Bellow's dear friend said to me in a low voice that she thought Tuck was "stupid." I nodded that I had heard her, not that I agreed, an ambiguous nod. I wished to be Bellow's biographer, but my heart was with Tuck in this: a school is for students, where they may ask all sorts of questions later perceived as stupid. Students do not limit themselves to brilliant questions, and I felt therefore that I should speak, defend Tuck.

But Tuck rescued himself by swiftly introducing a new subject. Kingman Brewster, president of Yale, had recently said that the Black Panthers could not receive a fair trial in New Haven. Did Bellow agree with that? Bellow said he had once eaten lobster with Brewster. I was pained for Tuck—how earnestly, how desperately he needed to know exactly what Henderson/Bellow believed about Africans in Connecticut! He read fiction to find out facts. He was frustratcd, stumped. I wanted to encourage Tuck without Bellow's feeling I was failing to support *him*. Bellow mustn't think of me as one of "the bullied elders of the faculty" sucking up to the young, swallowing my joyful saliva.

"I imagine," I said, "that if Brewster's recent views have changed it may have something to do with his son. For example, my own views have changed because of the convictions of my daughter Hester." I thought this was a mild and noncommittal statement.

Bellow declared that harmony between parent and child was impossible.

Tuck declared that it was his opinion as well as Brewster's that the Black Panthers could never receive a fair trial in New Haven.

Bellow said that he had not only had lobster with Kingman Brewster but that he thought Brewster "not intelligent."

Tuck declared that he himself was a liberal.

Bellow said, "It's awfully hard to talk to liberals." He added, "I could wear a button saying *Give Huey a Fair Trial* but I can't wear a button saying *Free Huey*. I can't advocate the overthrow of the federal judiciary system."

Tuck emphatically described the situation in Arkansas as he saw it. "I have uncles and other relatives who serve as judges in Arkansas, and they could never be fair in a trial between whites and blacks in any way touching on the black issue."

"I didn't say it was perfect," said Bellow. "I just said I won't overthrow the judiciary system."

Africa to Arkansas *via* New Haven. Tuck in search of Bellow's unequivocal convictions. But why should Bellow speak Tuckese? Tuck wanted an answer from Bellow in straight English, not in the language or license of fiction. He wanted Bellow to be his own translator. *Just where do you stand?* His demand was nothing so new. Black beard he might wear, rebel, liberator of the stultifying university, but he was asking the same old academic question, revealing the same old political, antiliterary weakness of which Bellow had already complained: "The university . . . is producing quantities of literary intellectuals who teach, write or go into publishing houses. So far as I can see this new group, greatly influenced by the modern classics, by Joyce, Proust, Eliot, Lawrence, Gide, Valéry, etc., have done little more than convert these classics into other forms of discourse, translating imagination into opinion, or art into cognitions. What they do is to put it all differently. They redescribe everything, usually making it less accessible. For feeling or response they substitute acts of comprehension."[5] Humboldt said it even more concisely: "Their business is to reduce masterpieces to discourse."

So Bellow refused to speak Tuckese, refused to tell where he stood. That is to say, he had told all, in his work, at which Tuck had glanced. His work was where he stood. What *chutzpah*, when you get all through his collected work you'll find that he didn't vote for anybody, that his characters did the voting, that Bellow subordinated himself to the law of the art of fiction, as if it were the federal judiciary.

Stony silence. The table awaited an answer. Someone mentioned that Nixon tonight would make a startling announcement, perhaps extending the war. It was not to be believed. A year before, protesting the war, upward of two hundred of our students had been arrested for disorder. Professor Hayman told how he and I, among others, dashed about raising bail for our jailed students. Bellow looked at me. Had I been a leader of that insubordinate mob? I said that I believed that those faculty (including several persons present at this table) who had assisted the arrested students had done a greater service for education than those faculty who condemned and abandoned the students.

Yet I was no longer where I had been a year before. To run around raising bail, yes, I would still do that. But in the intervening year I had known a certain psychological clarification, too—I had read a great deal of Bellow, and the most recent instrument of my clarification was Mr. Sammler, who had fled from Europe with his one eye remaining, leaving behind his wife in the grave he and she had dug together, shot to death by men and boys granted by their State the "prize of power . . . unobstructed enjoyment of murder." The enemy was disorder, ad hoc impromptu law, Left or Right. Bellow had written a remarkable sentence he would read tonight: "But loving kindness is often the favorite camouflage of the nihilist."[6]

5. "Cloister Culture," *The Best of "Speaking of Books,"* ed. Francis Brown (New York: Holt, Rinehart and Winston, 1969), p. 5.
6. "Culture Now," p. 178.

Self-indulgence, self-deception, frenzy. Add to these noble intentions and guns. Violence is a one-way route, all revolutions have ended in the same place. The enemy was guns, as Bellow had told me in the first moments I saw his face, at Tivoli in the first hour. Guns, guns, guns. Replace them with endless talk. Things will be better then. I could see it now as Bellow saw it. My reading of his work had carried me far forward. If I was not to be his biographer I would be at least his student, his reader, his literate explainer.

I THINK Bellow now liked me as he had not liked me before. I could be wrong. He felt that his brakes required adjustment. With his dear friend he followed me in his Mercedes-Benz to Imported Motors, across the river, in Lafayette. His car was ten years old. It was not Charlie Citrine's silver 280-SL Mercedes-Benz, which Cantabile demolished with baseball bats. The mechanic at Imported Motors promised to examine the brakes "soon as I can get to them." The afternoon was breathlessly close, and it would be long, too. Bellow was irritated. "I'm going back to Chicago tonight," he said, "if I have to run all the way."

"Soon as I can get to them," this Hoosier repeated.

On the other side of the river dozens of people would gladly have diverted Bellow for the afternoon. "Are we going to spend it at Imported Motors?" he asked. His mood was foul. He felt that his automobile was actually Eisinger's problem, since Imported Motors was Eisinger's garage. I was reminded of this departure from reason when I discovered Frank Tigler, husband to Humboldt's widow. Tigler and Citrine are fishing: "We were trawling from his boat," says Citrine, "and I was using his lure, so he said it was his trout." Citrine threw the fish in Tigler's lap.

Bellow's dear friend eased the moment by expressing the wish to see Ayre's department store. "Putting on Ayre's," said Bellow. We left Imported Motors in my Falcon. I said I had once owned a Japanese Toyopet. Bellow asked, "Did it have a slanted clutch?" At Ayre's he bought six three-cent stamps from a machine for twenty-five cents, complaining to a salesclerk, "The government is in a racket."

It occurred to Bellow, now that we had shopped at Ayre's, to buy a certain electric fixture for his apartment. He sought an "antique junk shop." In Ayre's I spied a friend. Bellow asked her where an antique junk shop might be found, and she recommended that we try the telephone directory. Bellow telephoned an auctioneer, who recommended Virgil Scowden at a nearby little town called Battle Ground. A famous battle occurred there. The world has been a battleground, but Bellow has never celebrated battle in fiction, as other writers often have. He does not have a desire to play soldier. His description of the Israelis and Arabs at war on parched and stinking battlegrounds do not encourage volunteers.

> Riding through the Sinai Desert, I thought it odd that so many canvas or burlap sacks should have fallen from passing trucks. I soon realized that these bursting brown sacks were corpses. Then I smelled them. Then I saw vultures feeding, and dogs or jackals. Then suddenly there was an Egyptian trench with many corpses leaning on parapets and putrefying, bare limbs baking in the sun like meat and a stink like rotting cardboard. The corpses first swelled, ballooned, then burst their uniform seams. They trickled away; eyes liquefied, ran from the sockets; and the skull quickly came through the face. Some readers, I thought, might wish to know what the aftermath of battle is like.[7]

Reverence for life comes first for Bellow, who celebrates animals, plants, trees, with his marvelous inexhaustible eye for the things of nature, their colors, their habits, their motions of life. To his account of two birds dead in a toilet at Ludeyville, Bellow brings more compassion than most writers bring to the deaths of boys or men at war. "A strange odor in the toilet bowl attracted his notice next, and raising the wooden lid he found the small beaked skulls and other remains of birds who had nested there after the water was drained, and then had been entombed by the falling lid. He looked grimly in, his heart aching somewhat at this accident."[8]

As we drove to Battle Ground he sank into his seat. He said he would survey Scowden's junk, and then we'd have a drink before the party. Certain returning memories lifted him for awhile from his listlessness. One of his wives had been from Lafayette—perhaps not a wife; perhaps a friend—and he recalled a Home for Soldiers nearby. Indeed, the instant he recalled it we came upon it in all its

7. "Reflections," *The New Yorker*, July 12, 1976, pp. 66–67.
8. *Herzog*.

dreary neglect, abandoned by America, visited by politicians during election campaigns. Bellow recalled certain relatives of his wife or friend, such as a man with a complicated name who, upon coming to America, simplified himself by adopting the name Lake Erie. He was known as Archie. Archie sold dehydrated applesauce. He ate garlic to improve his memory, but he led a miserable life and did not like what he remembered. An orthodox Jewish lady of the same family was mad for Clark Gebble, as she called him, and was in a terrible dilemma whenever religious duties interfered in any way with her opportunity to see a Gebble movie. Bellow quoted her in Yiddish—"How I love that Clark Gable!" But they were all dead, all that clan, he ticked them off, dead, dead, dead.

Scowden himself was not to be found, but we entered his shop and examined his junk, and we waited for him outside on chairs amidst a little grove of fuel tanks. Two old people lived in a small trailer attached to one of the fuel tanks. I am sure neither of the old people was to receive one thousand dollars for talking to anyone tonight. We became immobilized by a fine breeze from the river and sank into Virgil Scowden's junk chairs. It was the first and last cool air of the day. We dried out. Bellow's spirits improved. He wished tonight were over. He dreaded it. He knew that he would make fewer friends than enemies. Yet he had not come to win friends but to tell the thing he knew. He could have been amiable, told literary anecdotes, harmless lies—but in fact that was what he could not do. A speech was a form of writing, a series of thoughts or actions or mental events composed in private. The artist, Bellow would say tonight, quoting Collingwood, "tells the audience, at the risk of their displeasure, the secrets of their own hearts."[9] Tells and flees, off to Spain, Rome, Turkey, Block Island. Vanish. Tonight, back to Chicago.

Bellow's dear friend became tired. So did I. Foolishly, we left Scowden's yard, for soon we were damp again—clothing, car, air, the whole world was damp. Soon the river lay between him and his Mercedes-Benz. We went to my house for Josephine, and from our house Bellow telephoned Eisinger who, to my surprise, urged him to retrieve his car first, be late for the party. Thus we were abbreviating

9. "Culture Now," p. 178.

people's single opportunity to meet Bellow. Bellow telephoned Imported Motors, speaking angrily to someone there, and at the hour of the party we were driving instead back across the river through the quitting-time traffic, Bellow's bitterness toward Eisinger irrationally increasing. "Screw his fucking party," Bellow said, "he could have sent a graduate student to get my car."

Soon he achieved a calmer state. We arrived at Imported Motors. There stood his Mercedes. "Just where I left it," said Bellow, "nothing has been done to it." However, according to the honest mechanic, it *needed* nothing, and we drove back across the river to the Eisingers' house bursting with people, abundant with refreshment. Bellow and Eisinger warmly embraced. I could easily see why Eisinger himself could not have been expected to spend his afternoon negotiating with Imported Motors.

Since the banquet fare was notoriously poor (I did not find it so) it was the tradition of the English Department to eat and drink well beforehand. Bellow asked me to point out Mary Pat Gass. I directed him to her. She wore a polka-dot dress. Bellow was sucked into the crowd. I saw Mark Rowan, reaching over someone's shoulder, shaking hands with Bellow, and I heard Bellow say to the mathematician Meyer Jerison that he, Bellow, had once taken up calculus, but when his tutor told him that he *could* master it he gave it up with satisfaction.

THE LADY guarding the entrance to the Ballroom refused to admit Bellow without a ticket. Fortunately, however, Joel Burke was nearby, who led Bellow past the lady to the elevated speakers' table. Burke insisted that Bellow climb to the table, which Bellow in dismay recoiled from doing, for if he did he would be sitting in full view of hundreds of persons entering the Ballroom, alone, an object in a museum. Instead, he slumped to the stairway to the table, hiding his face in his hands. Someone thrust a book at him for his signature.

Each ticket-holder received a program decorated with an interesting woodblock by Bruce Woodford. Elsewhere in the program, however, lapses occurred of the kind uncharacteristic in a Department of English. The words "seize" and "donor" were misspelled. At a banquet honoring apprentice writers Bellow's two apprentice books ought not to have been unmentioned in the program. Publication date of *Seize the Day* was missed by nine years in a biography otherwise as charming as space permitted:

> Saul Bellow was born of Russian emigrant parents in Quebec in 1915. He moved to Chicago in 1924 and considers himself a Chicagoan "out and out." He studied at the University of Chicago, Northwestern University, and the University of Wisconsin. Of Chicago he has written: "The dense atmosphere of learning, of cultural effort, heavily oppressed me; I felt that wisdom and culture were immense and that I was hopelessly small." Mr. Bellow's reputation has grown steadily with the publication of a body of highly regarded major novels: *The Adventures of Augie March* (1953), *Henderson the Rain King* (1959), *Herzog* (1964), *Sieze the Day* (1956), and presently *Mr. Sammler's Planet*. Mr. Bellow is Professor of Letters and Literature and a member of the Committee on Social Thought at the University of Chicago.

Program.
Dinner.
Welcome, Joel Burke, chairman, Literary Awards Committee. Professor Burke told us that about sixty students had won prizes in writing ranging in sums from twenty-five dollars to one hundred dollars. These prizes would be awarded after Mr. Bellow had spoken. He dwelt amusingly on the students' lust for money, although it was my impression that in most cases the students had not written with money in mind. Indeed, on occasions like this I noticed that the faces of students winning merely Honorable Mention lighted up as if it were cash. So also Bellow, who had been a lowly student, Tuley High to the University of Wisconsin, heavily oppressed, hopelessly small, writing up his notions of the world long before anyone had given him reason to think there was money to be made out of such a propensity. When the time came that he was given money he accepted it as the reward for his labor, and if it was sometimes as much as a thousand dollars a night it may have been less in the long run than the fortune of the master mechanic at Imported Motors, or less than Virgil Scowden received for his junk.

The crowd was dense. Hundreds of people. Burke told me the figures afterward. So much food had heated us—roast beef, green beans, baked potatoes with sour cream, green salad, fruit salad, assorted pies, coffee. I drank many glasses of water poured from a sweating pitcher. Yet the heat increased.

Introduction of the speaker by Professor Chester Eisinger. Bellow read for seventy minutes after a minute or two of informal opening, wondering to start if he could live up to the generous "billing" of Professor Eisinger, loosening his bright cherry tie, adjusting his little Ben Franklin half-glasses above which he sometimes peered down at his dear friend sitting with Josephine and me below the speakers' table. Informally, too, not yet beginning, he could not help but optimistically observe that "the life of the mind survives in spite of the absurdities and barbarism of the twentieth century." In adjoining rooms, on television, Richard Nixon extending the war; so that it might have seemed futile to speak of books in a world of bombs except that one was always hopeful when one cared more for life than for death, standing right up there, giving his little talk to a congregation hoping to survive, "oddly faithful to things you learned as a boy," and so he began.

"I'm not sure," he said, "that what we have *is* a literary situation; it seems rather to be a sociological, a political, a psychological situation in which there are literary elements. Literature itself has been swallowed up. In East Africa last year I heard an account (probably sheer fantasy) of a disaster that had overtaken one of three young Americans who had parked their Land Rover under a tree for the night. A python had silently crushed and swallowed the young man. In the morning his friends saw the shape of his body within the snake and his tennis shoes sticking out of the creature's mouth. What we see of literature now are its sneakers.

"Why has this happened? No one should take on himself the responsibility of a definitive explanation—indeed, no such explanation would be generally acceptable—but, for what they may be worth, I am willing to offer my impressions and opinions. Literature became swallowable, enormously profitable, after World War II, thanks to the university boom, the expansion of the publishing industry and the new opportunities offered by journalism. In the universities a literary culture rapidly formed. It took charge of certain modern masterpieces (James, Lawrence, Joyce, Eliot, etc.), taught them, discoursed about them, *described* them. This process of re-description is most important. Everything was told again, in other

words, and related to myth, to history, to philosophy or to psychol-
ogy. Behind this body of interpretations appeared a new bureaucracy
with its own needs and ambitions and its own orthodoxy. Since the
masterpieces of modernism are radical, this orthodoxy is radical too.
. . . We have passed from contemplative reading to movement, to action, politics and power struggles. I do not mean large action, broad
movement or the conquest of national power. No, not large, not
broad. But intellectuals are curiously busy with social questions.
From the study of literature comes the prestige they enjoy and
exploit."

Bellow invites us to join him for "several miserable afternoons" at
the library. Here he has recently read—"forced myself"—certain
well-respected "literary magazines and the underground newspapers," old names, old friends, *Partisan Review*, *Playboy*. He reads
at length in the heating ballroom from Phillips. He reads from an
essay by Cecil Brown on "The White Whale." His eye seemed to
have caught it, he could not stop, though he had meant to illustrate
not his own unreason but Cecil Brown's.

"In *Playboy*, too, we can see the sneakers in the python's mouth"
—reading now from Leslie Fiedler: "Almost all today's readers and
writers," Fiedler said, "are aware that we are living through the
death throes of literary modernism and the birth pangs of postmod-
ernism." Modern literature "is *dead*. . . . The kind of criticism the
age demands is death-of-art criticism, which is most naturally prac-
ticed by those who have come of age since the death of the new poetry and the new criticism. It seems evident," Fiedler continued,
"that writers . . . must be reborn in order to seem relevant to the
moment and to those who inhabit it most comfortably: the young.
But one hasn't even the hope of being reborn unless he knows first
that he is dead."

"What a lot of death we have here," Bellow replies, reviewing.
"Ishmael is dead without knowing it. The survival of the Black man
will mean the death of America. The ship of the Great White Soul
sank in 1851 and since then we have been seeing post-mortem
effects. And now Fiedler's coroner's verdict. Actually he is nicer
than the others because he gives the dead a second chance. But what
a lot of ideological burial-parties the twentieth century has seen!
Common to them all is a certain historical outlook. All that is not
now, they say, is obsolete and dead. Any man who does not accept

the historical moment as defined by the only authoritative inter-
preters is dead. . . .

"Why does reading Fiedler's essay so promptly and strongly bring
fascism to mind? Is he really a dangerous person? Does he literally
mean that those of us who are over thirty-five might as well be
dead? Probably not. His job is to frighten us, to give us all a good
scare. . . . One can see why . . . *Playboy* goes for this. It is so bold, so
new, so spirited, so rebellious! But I shall not interrupt, I shall not
try to summarize. . . . In the old days he would have been writing
for the Hearst Sunday Supplement. (Hefner is quite a lot like W. R.
Hearst.) But hatred of liberalism, love of an imaginary past (Cow-
boys and Indians), somnambulistic certitude, praise of tribalism and
Dionysiac excesses, the cult of youth, the chastising of high culture
by the masses, the consecration of violence—all these suggest fascism. Lidless, the historical garbage can waits. . . . History is important for what you can get rid of. Considerations of style, quality, or
degree are irrelevant. According to Fiedler, we are confronted with
nothing less than the spiritual regeneration of mankind, we must
expect to pass through the earlier theological and metaphysical
stages of voodoo, storefront revivalism, astrology, holyrolling and
Manson cults. But the barbarous and monstrous will refresh us and,
as everybody knows, renewal always follows destruction. High culture will return—like *Mare Nostrum*? Like the Thousand-Year
Reich? . . .

"At this time, he says, we must yield and go along with pop art.
Does that mean that we must make terms with the media-manag-
ing intellectuals? Evidently it does. And here it begins to appear that
Dr. Fiedler's own class interests are involved. Isn't it obvious that
college-educated swinging, bearded, costumed, bohemianized intellectuals are writing the ads, manufacturing the gimmicks, directing
the shows, exploiting the Woodstocks? Dr. Fiedler, an influential ed-
ucator, is endorsing his own product. These new publicity intellectuals are his pupils. He tells us that the worst sins of the masses are
better than the dead virtues of high culture. From many beards we
hear amen to that. Yes, civilization has been profoundly disappointing. But this disappointment is also the foundation of their personal
success. *It*—civilization—is a failure, but *they*—the publicity intellectuals—are doing extremely well.

"What civilization has accumulated they treat as fuel and burn up. As the nineteenth century got its industrial power from coal, from the combustion of carboniferous forests, so successful operators burn up the culture of the nineteenth, the eighteenth, the seventeenth centuries, of all centuries of all the ages. While they complain of a consumer culture, they consume the past, consume it all. They see nothing wrong with this. They find their sanction in the Contemporaneous. For whatever is not Contemporaneous is worthless. Dead civilizations are to be cremated. Let us therefore have bigger bonfires, the bacchae out of their skulls courtesy of Dow Chemicals, whirling, while tribal music crashes from the amplifiers. Afterwards, peace and wisdom will return. Later."

I could never know exactly which portions of these readings, these remarks, so upset my lovely friend, Mrs. Wollan, or her friends, or my friends. Every ear heard its own vulnerability. Bellow had spoken at the risk of their displeasure against intellectuals smart enough to know they were sometimes exploitive, living on the boom, thriving upon discontent, and guilty consumers, too, bearded and swinging. Reading back, I am mystified. It all now seems so clear, that the "historical moment" was but a moment, that what we required was not death-of-art criticism but death-of-death, not a new Hearst in *Playboy* but a revived consciousness.

I saw, in the Ballroom, so many faces fall, friends of the young, friends of students, friends of that press and those writers Bellow condemned. I saw other people, antagonists of mine, perhaps in the long run right for wrong reasons. On the whole, faces falling, lovers of pop art, students of voodoo, activists who believed themselves at the opposite end of the spectrum from fascism, but it was Bellow's own life at stake, as it had been for Mr. Sammler, and he had come to tell the truth, if only for his own clarification; not to entertain, not to amuse—"This society, like decadent Rome, is an amusement society," reading, concluding. "That is the grim fact. Art cannot and should not compete with amusement. It has business at the heart of humankind. The artist, as Collingwood tells us, must be a prophet, 'not in the sense that he foretells things to come, but that he tells the audience, at the risk of their displeasure, the secrets of their own hearts. . . . No community altogether knows its own heart: and by failing in this knowledge a community deceives itself on the one subject concerning which ignorance means death. . . . The remedy is the poem itself. Art is the community's medicine for the worst disease of mind, the corruption of consciousness.'"[10] Here ending, whereupon the doors to the Ballroom were flung open, and the cooler air entered (or the warm air departed), and Bellow heard that applause which was respectful while admitting mystification, too, respectful of the weight, the sweat, the ardor, of the complexity undertaken, the task of telling what he knew to a world not always pleased to hear it, folding his papers for his pocket, folding his little Ben Franklin eyeglasses, nodding, bowing, smiling slightly, for this was not a gladiatorial show, neither was it a rally, and so he acknowledged the applause not with upraised arms but only by sedately nodding, bowing, and at the center of this moment saw beneath his chin several sheets of paper in quadruplicate attached to the hand of Assistant Professor Joel Burke, who insisted, knowing that Bellow would now leave the Ballroom—leave the campus, leave the city, leave the state—forced into Bellow's hand his own personal ballpoint pen with instructions to Bellow to sign the quadruplicated vouchers or forms or disclaimers or whatever they were which Burke for seventy minutes had clutched in anticipation of this single further minute. Bellow's face grew very red, and he signed, laughing, wherever Burke ordered him to sign, and passed from the Ballroom into the humid night to his little chance eavesdropping meeting on the sidewalk with Mrs. Wollan, who was so angry. Ladies had been angry with Bellow before. Nevertheless, he'd rather it were love.

10. Bellow's banquet reading is published as "Culture Now: Some Animadversions, Some Laughs," in *Modern Occasions*, Winter 1971, pp. 162–78. That text is offered here, much reduced in length. Certain material was added to the *Modern Occasions* text between the time of Bellow's reading and the time of publication. Interesting as that new material is, I have not included it here.

Chapter Nine

TIME ESCAPED. In 1968, back from my Chicago weekend, listless and cast down, I had thought I would accumulate seventy pages of Bellow notes and journal every year. In ten years I'd have seven hundred, enough to launch a book midway in the first term of Spiro Agnew. Things began predictably. Richard Nixon was elected president. Then again, reelected to a term he never finished, departing the White House one day in rivers of sweat, blessing his mother, and returning to the California seaside—he who had extended the war to Cambodia on the night of Bellow's speech condemning death.

But in ten years I had not many more pages than I'd had in 1968. I had a box full of notes, clippings, thoughts, citations from colleagues, packets of 3×5 cards in rubber bands. I was always intending to sort them out some day and get to work.

My family and I moved from Purdue to "Blau's school" in southern California. If Blau, according to Bellow, "should have begun with a couple of easy plays" at Lincoln Center he should have begun with modified ideals at the California Institute of the Arts, which became the last outpost of activism. Blau's toleration for perfect freedom for artists and for faculty exceeded the toleration of the Disney family, whose money it all was.

Therefore my family and I removed once more, back east, back into the country. If it was not Purdue it was the University of Pittsburgh. The venerable issues persisted. It was the commons room again, except that the Cathedral of Learning extended high into the city sky, not horizontal on the prairie; Mark Rowan was here, dead now, of tobacco, last seen shaking Bellow's hand over somebody else's shoulder in Chester Eisinger's bursting smoking living-room: every counterpart was here, everyone from everywhere, the same old crowd, the same old system, classes, colleagues, public meetings, private writings.

I felt myself approaching Bellow's wisdom. I could *feel* now certain things I had formerly known only through his books, his talk. I knew well enough by now the truth of his statement that writers seem nice enough until you get to know them. At Pittsburgh I was so nice to begin with that several young colleagues of mine who had done a bit of scribbling felt emboldened to tell me how I ought to conduct my classroom. They thought I was too permissive (at Blau's school the activists thought I was a monster of repression). I did not *assign* writing to students, I'd read what they wrote but I wouldn't force them to write, and my head flashed on Bellow in the Eisingers' living-room, "sick and tired of the progressive-school approach to writing—let's all put down our baseball gloves and write a poem." I was supportive of students, I never put *them* down, I never made them cry, never told them to quit. On the other hand, I did not attend their parties, their wine was too sweet, their smoke was too thick, their apartments were too cold, and the level of their noise too high. Yet I wondered if I had received this from Bellow or only from my own interior. Did I somehow know him or was I making him up? One day someone showed me an article revealing Bellow's similar method. The writer, Susan Dworkin, was telling of her experience with Bellow when he was a teacher visiting a writers' conference:

> For the most part Bellow said very little about our work. He seemed reluctant to make judgments or give too much guidance. [She] overheard Bellow say to someone that he always told young writers they were good. He hadn't the heart to do otherwise. They needed encouragement so much, much more than they needed hard criticism; he was scared by the need in their faces; he remembered his own need when he was young; he always told young writers they were good.[1]

Out of my Pittsburgh experience I wrote to him once at the tail of a long letter on another matter, "I think of you very often. I learned

1. "Saul Bellow and Me," *Ms*, March 1977.

a very great deal by reading you so intensely. You have informed my own way of life by telling me just a little bit in advance what one might be up against."

My novel, *The Goy*, appeared. Bellow had objected to the title. For that reason or another he never mentioned it to me, nor my autobiography, which I sent to him. Harold Rosenberg was dead, with whom we had driven in my Falcon from the Sterns' house to Naomi's party, Bellow at the wheel, Bellow tipping the doorman a dollar. Stern and Gay had separated. Susan and Daniel had moved from the South Side to the North Side without, as I heard, informing Bellow, who remarried and moved to the North Side, too. "I wish I could see you," I wrote to him on New Year's Day, 1976. "Surely you have urgent business in Pittsburgh," but he did not reply.

I heard from colleagues the circumstances of a visit Bellow made to Pittsburgh in 1959. These accounts—principally the narrative supplied by Richard Tobias—affected me in a significant way. "I once saw Bellow plain," Tobias wrote. "He was involved in a situation that nearly repeats the scene from his novel when Sammler goes to Columbia. In fact, as I sat in my seat at Stephen Foster Auditorium, I had the sensation that I had escaped from reality to be reborn into a novel." I began to feel that I ought to go ahead with the pages I had. Perhaps I too had seen Bellow plain—certainly plain enough for my purpose: the scene repeated, San Francisco, Columbia, Pittsburgh, Purdue, high expectations, an overflowing crowd, a difficult address, Q. and A., accusations of his having been boring, disappointing, effete, decrepit, rooted in his somehow violating expectations people had had no clear right to make in the first place. Professor Tobias continued:

> Bellow read a very academic lecture which he had written out in hand on legal-sized tablet. . . . He finished the lecture to respectable but not enthusiastic applause, and the chairperson said that Mr. Bellow had graciously agreed to answer questions from his audience.
>
> We sat in embarrassed silence. My mind was all abustle, but I could not think of any way to impose my attention on Bellow. Suddenly a young man in the balcony broke the ice for us.
>
> "Mr. Bellow, you have an international reputation as an artist, but tonight you have bored us to death. I counted twelve

people asleep and eight people who left before you had finished. Who cares about dull theory?"

In the shocked silence that lovely woman and excellent novelist herself Gladys Schmitt jumped to her feet to say the lecture stimulated her and excited her. Bellow began himself some defense: if the young man had wanted to be entertained, why hadn't he gone across the street where the Pirates were playing at Forbes Field. . . . I could feel some sympathy in the audience with the rude young man. Possibly the audience wanted Bellow to read parts of a new novel. Possibly the audience wanted gossip about writers and publishers. Maybe the audience wanted Bellow to diagram the way to write a successful novel.

The contretemps had nearly died down when one of our genuinely exciting graduate students, one who "thought about nothing but literature day and night," got to his feet. He thought that we ought to discuss a speaker's obligation to his audience. The Writers' Conference Director at that moment snatched the graduate student out of his seat and dragged him out to the lobby where we could hear them shouting at one another over the shouts at the ball game.[2]

I too could hear it. Bellow's reading. Moderate applause. A heavy silence. A voice from the balcony demanding to be liberated. Bellow's response refusing to perform. Perhaps I knew enough. I began to write. The poem "assumes direction with the first line laid down," wrote Robert Frost, from whom I drove directly to Bellow one summer day, 1961.

Encouraged by my own beginning I telephoned Stern to tell him I'd begun, it was time, I couldn't wait for more material, I'd need to go forward with what I had. Stern was reassuring, as he had so steadily been. "You can't wait forever to be right," he said. "Regarding character, everything is wrong *and* right." All that I thought I saw was there, I'd never know more, I'd never draw closer.

One month later I chose to write Bellow to tell him that I had at last begun my book. "I date this letter your birthday. It is one of the *hard* facts I have about you." It was ten years to the month since my

2. "'Audacious Ignorance and Timorous Knowledge': Saul Bellow's Noble Theme," Richard C. Tobias, University of Pittsburgh, an address, 1977.

letter to him from France, which somehow he never received, or so he said, the three of us standing there in our overcoats in some-body's apartment, waiting for Bonne Amie to return from another room. "This book," I wrote to Bellow, "is going to be interesting, re-liable, unique, kind, loving, appreciative, sound, intelligent, and ar-tistic. . . . It will not be a work at your expense. It will be as affectionate a book as anybody ever critically wrote about a friend or fellow-author, and I am hoping you will even request to see the manuscript ahead of time, so that you might catch me up at any point at which I might have injected a real problem or difficulty needlessly. . . ."

He might have begun by catching me up on the *hard* fact I'd got all wrong: his birthday was not July 10 but June 10, the day I had spoken to Stern. But he chose not to notice my error. Nor did he request to see my manuscript. He did not reply to my letter. Perhaps he never received it. How could I know?

Three months later I wrote to him again, this time in praise of his account of his visit to Israel, which had been printed serially in *The New Yorker*. It was there that he mentioned Oscar Wilde's "young man who had ruined himself through the vice of answering letters." This vice was not Bellow's. Nor did he reply to my short letter in the same month congratulating him on his having been awarded the Nobel Prize. "Of course I send you personally my greetings and con-gratulations," I wrote. "It's only the principle to which I object, the ugliness of competitiveness."

Indeed, the announcement of his winning the prize brought forth all sorts of expressions of hostility. Alfred Kazin wrote that "a visi-ble shudder ran through New York," a "vast tremor from the Village to Columbia, forced smiles, clenched teeth," possibly Kazin's shud-der, Kazin's tremor, smile, teeth. He quoted John Leonard of the New York *Times*: "If Saul Bellow didn't exist, someone exactly like him would have had to be invented just after the Second World War, by New York intellectuals, in a backroom at *Partisan Review*."[3] This is incorrect. No backroom committee—no committee of any sort—has wit enough or imagination to invent Bellow. Only Bellow could have invented Bellow, by hard solitary work over many years.

3. "Mr. Bellow's Planet," *New Republic*, November 6, 1976.

I think of Joel Burke at Purdue and the football boys I had tried to tell him about, practicing long afternoons.

On July 3 of the following year I wrote him once more, wishing him a happy Independence Day and lamenting my having missed him in Chicago on an occasion of my being there. He had gone off to Dallas. I enclosed a copy of an essay of mine on the prostate gland. Charlie Citrine in *Humboldt's Gift* cured his prostate problem by standing on his head, tightening his buttocks. He boasted afterward of "my amazingly youthful prostate." I suspected that Bellow had had some recent trouble along that line. I told him, too, that I had now completed my book about him. Neither of these subjects interested him sufficiently to cause him to reply.

THE GOSSIP of the papers was sometimes of Bellow's legal conflict with Susan. For more than a decade their conflict continued, an entanglement consuming souls and pockets while enriching lawyers. One was always hearing of marriages breaking. I remember taking Susan's word for it by telephone at the Del Prado Hotel. But this break took longer. Thirteen years later, after many judicial actions and hearings, the parties had achieved a deadlock.

One day the Pittsburgh *Press* announced that Bellow had been sentenced to jail "for falling $11,150 behind in alimony payments to his third wife." Third wife, no name for Susan. Another headline told me "Bellow sentenced," reporting the assertion of Susan's lawyer that "the novelist earned a total of $461,303 in 1976." My $60,000, of which I had boasted that night in the doorway of the restaurant, felt puny by comparison. In another day's paper I saw that Bellow was ordered to pay Susan $500,000 plus $800 a month, a sum soon reduced by the press to $200,000 in an article under the headline "Lowers the Boom on Bellow." A subsequent item made these events the occasion of a pun—"Ignoble Prize."

Was Bellow to be sent to jail? I depended upon Stern to keep me informed. He explained to me that it was all "legal strategy," a plan whereby, in the light of real circumstances, as opposed to lawyers' notions of Bellow's wealth, Bellow's responsibilities would be scaled to his resources.

It entered my head, however, that if Bellow were sent to jail I would visit him there. He could not run off to Dallas, plead indiges-

tion, plead a lost wallet, nor plot his escape with friends in secret
Chicago language. Confined, he'd be glad enough to see me, I'd be
better company than the brutal guards. I had several questions to
ask him which I'd never asked. "Why all this remarrying?" That was
one. If it doesn't work after, say, the second time, why not quit? "Is
marriage a crisis for you, as courage was for Hemingway?" I wanted
to know more about his teaching, and how he managed to remain so
long at one university. How did he *do* the teaching? Did he lecture
or was he more discussion-leader? I had no idea of his classroom procedure, and I was anxious to pump him on the subject. In my
thoughts, as I grilled him he sat on a wooden stool in a corner of his
cell pondering my questions, and I with my Flair and my note-pad
taking down his answers. In my daydream I had cornered the
woodchuck.

In *Humboldt's Gift* in passages of brilliance Bellow struck at the
heart of the matter. To Judge Urbanovich in Chicago the economics
of the novelist was a mystery as deep as the art itself. If art was "the
community's medicine" the Judge wanted none of it. He treated Bellow like any other man with an income in six figures, perceiving no
difference between the energies of a writer and the energies of any
other economic enterprise. The infinite mind of an artist is but a
finite resource, incapable of infinitely and endlessly producing
goods like a factory: not all the backroom committees in the world
could work the head of Bellow; no workers on the nightshift, no
family or associates carry on when the head sleeps.

Charlie Citrine appears with his lawyers in the chambers of Judge
Urbanovich, "plump and bald, a fatty, and somewhat flat-faced. But
he was cordial, he was very civilized. He offered us a cup of coffee. I
referred his cordiality to the Department of Vigilance . . ."

> "We've now had five sessions in court," Urbanovich began.
> "This litigation is harmful to the parties—not to their law-
> yers, of course. Being on the stand is frightful for a sensitive
> person like Mr. Citrine. . . ." The judge meant me to feel the
> ironic weight of this. Sensitivity in a mature Chicagoan, if
> genuine, was a treatable form of pathology, but a man whose
> income passed two hundred thousand dollars in his peak years
> was putting you on about sensitivity. Sensitive plants didn't

make that kind of dough . . . "Your problem, Mr. Citrine, is your proven ability to earn big sums."

"Not lately."

"Only because you're upset by the litigation. If I end the litigation, I set you free and there's no limit to what you can make. . . . It's inconceivable, whatever happens, for Mr. Citrine ever to fall below the fifty-percent tax bracket. So if he pays Mrs. Citrine thirty thousand per annum it only costs him fifteen thousand in real dollars. Until the majority of the littlest daughter."

"So for the next fourteen years, or until I'm about seventy, I must earn one hundred thousand dollars a year. I can't help being a little amused by this, your Honor. Ha ha! I don't think my brain is strong enough, it's my only real asset. Other people have land, rent, inventories, management, capital gains, price supports, depletion allowances, federal subsidies. I have no such advantages."

. . . But the judge was giving me a going-over, reinterpreting the twentieth century for me, lest I forget, deciding how the rest of my life was to be spent. I was to quit being an old-time artisan and adopt the methods of soulless manufacture. . . . Suddenly my detachment ended and I found myself in a state. I understood what emotions had torn at Humboldt's heart when they grabbed him and tied him up and raced him to Bellevue. The man of talent struggled with cops and orderlies. And, up against the social order, he had to fight his Shakespearian longing, too—the longing for passionate speech. This had to be resisted. I could have cried aloud now. I could have been eloquent and moving. But what if I were to burst out like Lear to his daughters, like Shylock telling off the Christians? It would get me nowhere to utter burning words. The daughters and the Christians understood . . . the judge didn't. Suppose I were to exclaim about morality, about flesh and blood and justice and evil and what it felt like to be me, Charlie Citrine? Wasn't this a court of equity, a forum of conscience? And hadn't I tried in my own confused way to bring some good into the world? Yes, and having pursued a higher purpose although without even getting close, now that I was aging, weakening, disheartened, doubting my endurance and even my sanity, they wanted to harness me to an even heavier load for the last decade or so. Denise was not correct in saying that I blurted out whatever entered my head. No sir. I crossed my arms on my chest and kept my mouth shut, taking a chance on heartbreak through tongueholding."

ONE DAY I who for thirteen years had hoped to become Bellow's biographer, Bellow's confidant, to whom he would open and reveal all the secret files of his heart (not to mention royalty statements, tax returns, business correspondence, literary correspondence, and love letters), heard from colleagues of a notice in the *New York Times Book Review*: "For an authorized biography of Saul Bellow, I would appreciate receiving any letters, documents, anecdotes, personal memoirs and photographs from his friends and associates."

The letter was signed by Ruth Miller, living on Lower Sheep Pasture Road in East Setauket, New York, but whether she was wholly its author I was never certain. I tried to reach Bellow by telephone. Luckily I failed. I was angry. Why had I been dumped for this—who was she? I telephoned Stern and explained what I had seen. He was mystified. "I never heard of her," he said. At the *New York Times Book Review* an employee who seemed to be well informed said I knew as much as she. The letter belonged to a category called "Authors' Queries." She could hardly tell me more. Could it be a printing error, I asked. Authorized by whom? Did the *Times* check out this possible authorization? "It *could* have been a printing error," the employee said, such things happen. "They're mailed in and we take people at their word and run them when we have space. We basically believe what people say."

I wrote quickly to Miller herself, telling her of my own long-standing hope to become, as she now had, Bellow's authorized biographer. "You must have something I don't have," I wrote.

She promptly replied: "First let me apologize for the New York Times announcement." She was writing, she said, not biography but a "literary study along the lines of my study of Emily Dickinson. There is no authorized biographer or biography, certainly not now, and from me, no way. I couldn't possibly undertake anything of that sort. I have known Saul since 1938 and our meetings over the years have only the books as the subject between us." My indignation subsided.

A COLLEAGUE of mine from Pittsburgh, removing himself and his family to a new life at Athens, Georgia, showed my manuscript of my experience of Bellow to the editor of *The Georgia Review*, an elegant and high-minded journal that has been publishing work of literary interest for more than thirty years. When the editor read my manuscript he became enthusiastic, asking me if he might print an excerpt; I in turn was enthusiastic, and we settled on a section of the manuscript to be published as "Saul Bellow at Purdue." We explained in a headnote to readers that "the comedy spread below is part of a larger work."

For this excerpt I required Bellow's permission to reprint certain work and correspondence. I would write to him. Since he had not replied to my recent letters I was not especially optimistic about his replying now. On the other hand, in his last letter he *had* granted me permission to reprint a story of his in an anthology edited by my wife, my daughter, and me. His letter had the characteristic sound of his manner of adjusting to me—perhaps to others as well: it was a brief, layered letter, first scolding, next kindness, and finally a good laugh:

> It seems to me that if the Harris family does an anthology it does its own anthology without benefit of publisher's advice and that if you fall out with T. Y. Crowell Company you find another publisher. Since you are inclined to capitulate to an editor and are changing the title of your book to *Harris Family and Editor's Anthology* you have my permission to reprint "The Gonzaga Manuscripts." You have worn me out. This is not quite the same as winning your point. I think you will now need the Viking Press permission to use the story. I wouldn't dream of writing my own autobiography. There would be nothing much to say except that I have been unbearably busy ever since I was circumcised.

Now, for my *Georgia Review* excerpt, he once again obliged me with a response. "I don't much mind if you quote me, though my editing finger itches. But I realize it's not right to edit one's own letters. They are what they are." The excerpt when printed apparently pleased or amused people. It "drew a heavily favorable response," one editor wrote, "and helped to boost sales for that issue (Winter 1978) to the point where we were virtually out of print only a few weeks after publication (even though we had increased our press run in anticipation of likely demand)."

Bellow, on the other hand, cared very little for it, beginning with the drawings by David Levine on the cover: Bellow had not cared for them in the past and did not care for them now. This made me nervous. The drawings, which I had never seen, echoed my text: to dislike the drawings would be to dislike the text. There were three drawings, catching Bellow as the casual eye might catch him—first jaunty, small cap set upon brains; next, his head buried in torrents of mail, and finally Bellow crucified but amiable, as if, when pressed, he'd confess it wasn't he who was crucified but the world of human pain for which he had tried to speak in the voices of Citrine, Bummidge, Henderson, and others.

One day I telephoned him on the North Side. His wife answered. Her accent was European. Stern had told me that Bellow had recently been relatively serene. He sounded so to me. Stern had also mentioned Bellow's being "unhappy" about my excerpt. "Dick told me you were unhappy about it," I said.

His serenity lessened. "I thought I looked like a turd in it," he impatiently said.

I was astonished. "Really?" It was all I could ask.

"Yup," he replied. "Bad-tempered. Nasty, Snappish. I don't see myself that way."

"That's because it's not oneself," I awkwardly said. "It's my version of oneself."

"Biography," said Bellow memorably, "is a specter viewed by a specter."

I mentioned Ruth Miller, whose letter had been in the *Times*. "No, that was a mistake," he said. "Somebody's just writing about my writing, not about my life. The less I see about my life the better."

I asked him if he had heard that I was soon to publish the whole book from which the excerpt had come. No, he hadn't heard. "So I've been thinking," I said, "we might have just one more meeting so I can ask a few questions and jot a few things down. I promise you that when this book is off I'll never again write another thing about you."

"You sound as if you're about to take a pledge," he said.

"I hear you're going to speak in Milwaukee," I said—this was a symposium called "The Autobiographical Mode: New Ideas of the Self." "I thought I might drop up," I said.

"You're not on the program?" he inquired.

"No," I said, "but Blau is, and I haven't seen him in a long time, and I haven't seen you in even longer."

"I'm a little more used up than last time," he said.

"I thought we might spend a little time together," I suggested.

"You and Blau?"

"You and I. I thought I might go up through Chicago . . . maybe drive up from Chicago together . . ."

"You know," said Bellow, "you have a perfect right to do what you like with your observations but I don't see that you can expect me to extend myself to provide you with brickbats."

Had I thrown brickbats?

"What you write about me," said Bellow, "is entirely your own choice, but why do you ask me to collaborate, to *volunteer*?"

"Then you won't be socially available in Milwaukee," I suggested.

"I'm just going there and give my talk and leave," he said.

"I hear that you're writing a book," I said.

"I haven't got the time to give it up there."

"I hope the book is coming well," I said. "I can see very clearly that you don't care to linger in public."

"No I don't," he said. "I stay covered over."

I DECIDED not to go to Milwaukee. I lay in wait in Pittsburgh where he would soon arrive for a grand lecture under the sponsorship of the International Poetry Forum. I consulted with Samuel Hazo, poet, writer, director of the International Poetry Forum, at his office in Carnegie Library. The spines of his books were familiar—Bellow's books—for Hazo was to introduce Bellow from the platform when he appeared. Thus he was reading him now. Very sensible. Had Bellow, I asked, specifically *requested* that Hazo introduce him? Had he, I meant, specifically ruled out anybody else?

As a matter of fact, said Hazo, it was odd. Bellow indicated—well, not Bellow but Bellow's secretary, for Hazo himself had never spoken to Bellow directly nor received a letter actually from Bellow. They had never met. It was all done through Bellow's secretary and through the mediation of Joseph Epstein, editor of *The American Scholar*, who was a friend of both.

Bellow wouldn't have agreed to come at *all*, said Hazo, except that he had a friend in Pittsburgh. "That's the only reason he'll come. This friend. He wouldn't come otherwise." Hazo could not recall the name of Bellow's friend. It was in his letter. In his secretary's letter. But he hadn't the letter, and he couldn't be sure that the friend had actually been named.

Hazo could remember only that Bellow's friend was a lady eye doctor. Maybe Bellow's secretary mentioned her name on the phone, unless it was Epstein who mentioned it.

I was unacquainted with any lady eye doctors in Pittsburgh. And yet, how many could there be? The yellow pages of the telephone directory showed several columns of eye doctors, many of them identified by initials, from M. J. Abramson to J. W. Zelazowski. I could begin, I supposed, to telephone them one by one. It was awkward, inviting rebuff and rejection. "May I speak to the eye doctor, please, if she is a woman." The doctor takes the line. She is an eye doctor, she is a woman, is she also an old friend of Saul Bellow?

Instead, however, I purchased three tickets to Bellow's lecture. It was ten years to the month since he had come to Purdue. I attended with Josephine, our son Henry, Professor Richard Tobias, and Tobias's wife, Barbara. Tobias had been among the audience for Bellow at the Stephen Foster Auditorium twenty-one years before, across the street from the clamor of Forbes Field. Bellow, introduced now by Hazo, declared that he would read, not lecture. "We are all lectured to enough," he said.

Beautifully he read his story, "A Silver Dish," for an hour and a quarter for six hundred people. Then shyly, awkwardly, wordlessly, lost, uncomfortable, compelled by circumstance to traverse alone and unescorted a sizeable space between the lectern and the wings, waving, sheepish, trying to smile, he disappeared—he who through his writings had enriched me and amused me and informed me, raised up my consciousness, deepened my sense of myself as writer and as citizen of the planet. But I took no notes, having taken a pledge.